Beth -

a great pleasure
to meet you - I hope
that enjoy my work

kind regards

24 June 2011

THE MASTER ARCHITECT SERIES

keith williams

Architecture of the Specific

images
Publishing

Published in Australia in 2009 by
The Images Publishing Group Pty Ltd
ABN 89 059 734 431
6 Bastow Place, Mulgrave, Victoria 3170, Australia
Tel: +61 3 9561 5544 Fax: +61 3 9561 4860
books@imagespublishing.com
www.imagespublishing.com

National Library of Australia Cataloguing-in-Publication entry:

Title:	Keith Williams : architecture of the specific.
ISBN:	978 1 86470 235 4 (hbk.)
Notes:	Includes index.
Subjects:	Williams, Keith, 1958 April 21-
	Keith Williams Architects.
	Architects – Great Britain.
	Architecture, Modern – 21st century.

Dewey Number: 720.92

Coordinating editor: Andrew Hall

Digital production by the Graphic Image Studio, Pty Ltd, Australia
www.tgis.com.au

Digital production by Chroma Graphics (Overseas) Pte Ltd, Singapore
Printed on 150 gsm Quatro Silk Matt by Everbest Printing Co. Ltd., Hong Kong/China

IMAGES has included on its website a page for special notices in relation to this and our other
publications. Please visit www.imagespublishing.com.

Front cover photography: The Long House, copyright Hélène Binet
Back cover photography: Keith Williams, copyright James Cameron

Contents

Keith Williams is design director of Keith Williams Architects. The London-based firm, which he founded in 2001, has won more than 20 major design and construction awards and has twice been winner of the BD Public Building Architect of the Year Award, in 2006 and 2008.

Born in 1958, Williams studied architecture initially at Kingston and subsequently at Thames (now Greenwich) schools of architecture, gaining honours in both his degree and postgraduate diploma. On qualifying as an architect in 1983, he worked firstly for Sheppard Robson and then for Terry Farrell & Partners. He co-founded Pawson Williams Architects in 1987 and went on to establish Keith Williams Architects in 2001.

Keith Williams is a Fellow of the Royal Society of Arts, a member of the Royal Institute of British Architects and of the Royal Institute of the Architects of Ireland. He sits on the National Design Review Panel of the Commission for Architecture and the Built Environment. He has judged numerous international architectural competitions and architectural awards programs and has been visiting critic and guest lecturer at many schools of architecture. Williams has been the winner of a significant number of national and international architectural competitions and his work has been published worldwide.

He is married and lives and works in London.

On Architecture

'In Architecture there is a part that is logical, pragmatic, reasoned, and there is a part that emerges from the sensual and the aesthetic. Without a collision between these opposing principles it seems unlikely that great architecture can ever be made.'

Keith R Williams

Keith Williams with co-director Richard Brown

Williams' buildings are shaped by his core belief that architecture is primarily concerned with simple components such as light, form, space, scale, material and context. It is up to the architect to use his or her skills to determine the way in which these things are combined that will have the capability to enthral and enrich the experience of people who are touched by them.

Awards

2009

RIAI Awards 2009: Best Cultural Building
Wexford Opera House
Award Winner

RIBA Awards 2009
Wexford Opera House
Award Winner

Irish Times Special Jury Award
Wexford Opera House
Award Winner

2008

OPUS Awards
Wexford Opera House
Award Winner

BD Public Building Architect of the Year
Keith Williams Architects
Award Winner

Chicago Athenaeum International Architecture Prize
Unicorn Theatre
International Award Winner

RIBA Awards 2008
The Long House
Award Winner

World Architecture News House of the Year
The Long House
International Finalist

2007

Copper in Architecture Awards 13
Unicorn Theatre
UK Award Winner

RIAI Awards: Best House Award
The Long House
National Award Winner

USITT Award
Unicorn Theatre
Award Winner

2006

BD Public Building Architect of the Year
Keith Williams Architects
Award Winner

Stirling Prize Nomination (Penultimate Round)
Unicorn Theatre
Shortlisted

RIBA Awards 2006
Unicorn Theatre
Award Winner

Chicago Athenaeum International Architecture Prize
Athlone Civic Centre
International Award Winner

RIAI Awards 2006: RIAI Overseas Award
Unicorn Theatre
Award Winner

Irish Concrete Society Awards 2006
Athlone Civic Centre
Overall Award Winner

AAI Awards 2006
Athlone Civic Centre
Special Mention

2005

Opus Architecture & Construction Awards
Athlone Civic Centre
Award Winner

RIBA Awards 2005 RIBA European Award
Athlone Civic Centre
Award Winner

RIAI Awards 2005: Special Award
Athlone Civic Centre
Award Winner
Best Sustainable Project

RIAI Awards 2005
Athlone Civic Centre
Award Winner

Lighting Design Awards 2005
Athlone Civic Centre
Award Winner

2004

Richmond Society Awards: Gold Medallion
Orange Tree Theatre
Winner

Foreword
by Paul Finch

Architecture has both an interior life and an exterior impact, a private world and a public face; that is why architecture is a political as a well as a social art. In Britain, the task of retaining design integrity given the complexities of politics, the planning system, procurement regimes, heritage groups and other taste arbiters is not an easy one. The elephant traps set by those suspicious of 'modernistic' architecture are legion. It sometimes seems near miraculous that serious contemporary architecture manages to emerge at all.

So it comes as a pleasant surprise to find an architect, Keith Williams, who has managed to build without compromise (beyond the necessary design iterations required to produce any good building), in a way that is neither bombastic nor unnecessarily reticent. The practice's many projects and commissions, both within and beyond the UK, range across both scale and building type. All have resulted in designs that deal consistently with the elements informing good architecture: space, light, movement, materiality and, in particular, public realm.

You will find in the pages that follow examples of completed work, competition entries, one-off projects and work in progress that provide encouraging evidence of clients and planners treating architecture as an adult activity. No doubt that is partly because much of the work, but not all, is concerned with cultural commissions rather than the more contentious worlds of commerce and industry, but the insertion of new cultural buildings into existing contexts is no easy matter.

What Keith Williams has managed to do is to combine functional, psychological and aesthetic considerations in respect of the interior life of the building, with a considered and convincing attitude to the urban settings in which he mostly works. The resulting architecture, a combination of interior complexity and external simplicity, is impressive.

The most extreme example of this combination is the Wexford Opera House; at ground level one would scarcely imagine that such a building could have been fitted on to a tiny backland site. Its significance in urban terms can only be fully understood from a distance, where the necessary vertical expression of an opera house (the flytower) marks the building as a key element in the city.

This sort of architecture is not just the provision of a new street address. It works its way into the grain of a place, and because in this case the building has a public use, the architecture takes on an added significance. It is concerned with interiors and with public effect, but it has also become part of the interior life of the city itself.

Architecture like this is not so easy to find.

Paul Finch is editor emeritus of The Architectural Review *and programme director of the World Architecture Festival*

Athlone Civic Centre

Architecture of the Specific:
The Romantic Rationalism of Keith Williams
by Kenneth Powell

At a time when the British architectural scene appears to be drifting towards a new Puritanism, a clear reaction against the expressive and the 'iconic' form-making tendencies of the last decade or so and a trend relieved only by outbursts of the purely fanciful or the weakly decorative, the architecture of Keith Williams stands out as a reasoned and rational restatement of perennial architectural values. Equally, in a period of economic trauma when the value of much generated by the last era of boom is being questioned, the strength of Williams' work lies in its endorsement of even more venerable architectural truths – permanence, solidity, even monumentality, and a taste for the richness that comes from the use of fine materials. The ethos in which Williams operates is not one of throw-away buildings. He brings a sense of timeless permanence to his work. It is symptomatic, perhaps, that he has so far done little in the field of speculative development and that so many of his projects involve substantial improvements to the wider public domain.

Williams' emergence as a leading light in what might be called the middle generation of British architects – he qualified in 1983 – has been a gradual process. There was no single dramatic competition win (so many of them end in disillusion), no one star project that marked his rise to the front ranks. Rather he has assembled through a series of competition successes – competing often against international stars such as Chipperfield, Eisenman, Ando and Holl – a portfolio of very significant civic and cultural projects that have allowed him to pursue his passionate exploration of form, space, light, materiality and procession. Significantly younger than the ex-Foster and Rogers alumni who were the key figures in remaking the British scene during the 1980s, Williams trained at Kingston, the school which, a few decades earlier, had produced the legendary partnership of Chamberlin, Powell & Bon. Kingston was itself a significant influence, offering a training divorced from the fancies of the AA and unconstrained by the literal modernism of Cambridge – for the roots of the new Puritanism, look no further than Leslie Martin. Williams recalls the school as 'a hothouse of intellectually opposing ideas, with the rationalism of Aldo Rossi crashing into the work of a resurgent Michael Graves'.

From Kingston, Williams studied at Greenwich School of Architecture and then went to work (briefly) for Sheppard Robson before joining the office of Terry Farrell. Farrell was then making waves with a series of big London projects that reflected the influence of American Postmodernism. The Farrell project in which Williams was most closely involved was, however, very different from Embankment Place (though he was involved with the early stages of that scheme) or Vauxhall Cross. Indeed, Regatta Headquarters at Henley on Thames remains one of the most satisfying of Farrell's buildings.

Though Williams himself was never strongly attracted by Postmodernism as a style, he was impressed, he says, by the 'intensity' of the Farrell office and 'the fact that we were exploring the spaces between buildings which, Farrell rightly felt, were as important as the buildings themselves'. This notion became a formative influence on Williams' subsequent work. By the age of 29, Williams had moved on to launch his own practice in partnership with Terry Pawson (another Kingston alumnus who went to work for Farrell). The practice lasted more than a decade but in contrast to many professional partnerships, it ended reasonably amicably – if with a sense on both sides, perhaps, that it had gone on too long.

There had been some notably successful projects, including the Earth Galleries at London's Natural History Museum and the remodelling of the Birmingham Repertory Theatre, Williams' first theatre project. But Williams felt the need to form his own team and pursue his own ideas and so Keith Williams Architects was launched in 2001, working initially from the old Pawson Williams office in Covent Garden but more recently from a converted warehouse on the fringes of Bloomsbury. It's a calm place, with an air of concentration and intense creativity, littered with cardboard study models of current or discarded ideas. Williams – now with Richard Brown as a fellow director – remains very much a team leader, with a firm hand on everything that the office does. 'I see myself as instigator, critic and overseer, shaping the architecture as it emerges and refining the resultant outputs', he says. Williams' drawings and sketches (each fastidiously dated to chart precisely in time when key design directions were established) are the starting point for all the practice's projects, developing into both physical and computer-generated models as the next stage in the emergence of a scheme.

Asked about key influences on his work, Williams comes up with unsurprising names – Le Corbusier and Louis Kahn, in particular. Both were supreme creators of space, and it is this characteristic that emerges so strongly in Williams' own architecture. Tadao Ando, James Stirling, Aldo Rossi and, more distantly, Nicholas Hawksmoor are also cited among Williams' 'giants', while the work of David Chipperfield, the Irish school of De Blacam & Meagher and O'Donnell & Tuomey and the vibrant Swiss scene have all fed into his thinking. Attempt a synthesis of these hugely varied influences and you might end up with something loosely described as romantic rationalism – not a bad description of Keith Williams' recent work. There is always a strong physicality to a Williams building. His architecture is emphatically not that of the glass box – masonry, he says, 'is quite a good material to build with' and the way in which the solid wall is used is key to Williams' 'box of tricks' (a term he took from a lecture by Denys Lasdun, another source of inspiration. He is a great admirer of that 'flawed masterpiece', the National Theatre). Williams confesses to briefly toying with 'blobs and arbitrarily funky shapes' – just to ensure he wasn't missing something, perhaps – but 'they don't really do it for me', he says. Nor are there any obvious connections in Williams' work with the British High-tech school, though he admires the degree to which Richard Rogers perennially incorporates significant public spatial gestures into so many of his projects.

The idea of a technically driven architecture is, indeed, alien to Williams. He finds inspiration in the other arts, painting and sculpture, in the work of artists like Rachel Whiteread and Richard Wilson (both have a strongly architectural instinct). Composition is fundamental to his architecture. Williams talks of the necessity for an architect to 'establish the ground rules'. 'You have to define your own critical position', he says. In his case, this process has been long and hard. But now the work seems to have reached a calm maturity, with a promise of new territory to be explored and won.

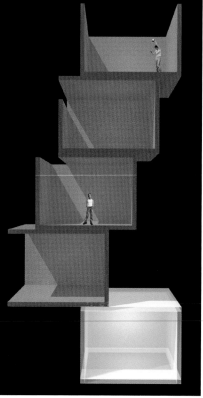

Lighting model, Sculpture Building, Royal College of Art

Given Keith Williams' keen interest in the arts, including theatre, music (opera in particular) and dance, it is not surprising that performing arts buildings, as well as museums and galleries, figure prominently among both his completed oeuvre and his unbuilt projects. A number of theatre projects followed on from Williams' work at the Birmingham Rep. The extension to the Orange Tree Theatre in Richmond, Surrey (2002–03) was a modest job in most respects – the budget was just £400,000 – but is a skilful and sensitive addition to an established urban scene that also provides much-needed amenities (rehearsal, workshop and storage space) for this popular local venue. It embodies Williams' belief that 'arts buildings can make a huge difference to the life of communities'. Winning the competition to design the new Unicorn Theatre on London's South Bank was a shot in the arm for Williams' newly formed practice. The site was located on Tooley Street, Southwark, on the edge of the huge More London office development. A narrow line of retained, and now restored, 19th-century buildings extends along the eastern end of Tooley Street, providing a striking counterpoint to the big office slabs behind. The new theatre, opened in time for Christmas 2005, forms a bookend to the block, with the narrow Unicorn Passage (the line of which was retained in the More London masterplan) to the west, offering distant glimpses of the river. To complete the job, as it were, Williams is now working on an adaptation of the listed 19th-century former fire station directly opposite the Unicorn, the two buildings framing, as unequal sentinels, the pedestrian route from Tooley Street to the Thames.

Shetland Cinema and Music Venue

The Unicorn is not only the first entirely new theatre built in London in many years but also, unusually, a theatre specifically designed for children, providing a permanent home for a company that began its existence more than 60 years ago touring in a couple of ex-army trucks. For some architects, the nature of the audience would form the building – condescension, whimsy, even sentimentality would creep in. And the children would be the first to find all that wearisome. Williams' Unicorn is a building for children, but not a childish building. It's only gradually that you notice the way in which elements of it are scaled down to the needs of small people – the handrails on the stairs, for example, or the windows at low level. The main auditorium is a delight, intimate and intense – a place to be enthralled. But the real drama of the building – and drama there is, in the architecture as well as the activities it contains – is generated by the constraints of the tight site, producing a highly vertical structure. The double-height foyer is an impressive space, and the main auditorium sits on top of it – the lack of obvious structure is the result of collaboration between Williams' office and Arup engineers. The auditorium box projects out over Unicorn Passage to maximise available space, and the massive concrete stair stack appears to be supported by nothing – a hint of Williams' mannerist leanings – providing a classic instance of the promenade architecturale of which he is so fond.

One of the delights of the building, which was shortlisted for the penultimate round of the RIBA's Stirling Prize, is the high quality of materials and finishes (stone floors and walnut joinery, for example) – quite an achievement given the relatively modest budget. The Unicorn reflects a theme that recurs in Williams' projects: a very successful architect/client relationship, in this instance with the theatre's artistic director, Tony Graham, who brought in groups of local schoolchildren to make their input to the development of the brief. 'Tony's original brief', Williams recalls, 'was, while confessing little knowledge of architecture, to create a building that was "rough yet beautiful"'.

The Unicorn was certainly a factor in Keith Williams' success in the competition for the new Wexford Opera House, but there are other theatre projects. The Marlowe Theatre in Canterbury, located on the fringe of the cathedral city's World Heritage Site, looks set to be another example of Williams' ability to squeeze maximum value out of a limited budget. The Marlowe is a highly successful regional venue, currently housed in a cheaply converted 1930s cinema. Williams' project demolishes the existing theatre, save for the stage and the structural bones of the fly tower – their retention effectively defines the plan of the new theatre. The seating capacity of the main auditorium, on a horseshoe plan, and lined with strips of timber, will be increased from 900 to 1200, with a new 150-seat performance space at upper level, cafés and bars, rehearsal space and much enhanced backstage facilities included in the reconstruction. Construction of the new theatre began in May 2009.

Williams' concern to integrate buildings with public space is reflected in the external treatment of the building, with the sweeping curve of the new foyer reinforcing the street edge with an 8-metre-tall colonnade that relates to the scale of nearby buildings. There was considerable debate locally about the impact of the new theatre on the city skyline – 'the fly tower was a big issue', Williams says. 'Functionally it had to remain, so in order to improve its silhouette we increased its height and sculpted it into a pinnacle'. The fly tower is the tallest structure in the centre of Canterbury, after the 'Bell Harry' central tower of the cathedral, and to propose increasing its height was a bold – and controversial – move. The fly tower will be clad in stainless steel mesh, a material that shimmers in the light and reduces the apparent bulk of the structure. The small auditorium is clad in copper. This is a scheme, pragmatic but stylish and with clear community benefits, that suggests the probable future of arts projects in Britain, at least in the next decade or so, now that Lottery cash is in short supply and the £50–100 million projects of the millennium era are becoming a distant memory. At the same time Williams craves the challenge of a really big arts project. Amongst the most notable of his 'unbuilts' (and the largest scheme his office has worked on to date) is the premiated competition scheme of 2001 for the Centro Culturale in Turin, containing a 32,000-square-metre public library and 1800-seat auditorium, topped by a rooftop garden, and designed to have something of the civic impact that Piano & Rogers' Pompidou Centre had on Paris. Williams envisaged the building as 'a palazzo to knowledge, open to all, in a city famous for its great private palazzi'.

Ireland has featured prominently in Williams' career to date. His was one of the very few British practices to have benefited from the boom in civic building in that country over the last decade, the result of devolution and the restructuring of local government in the context of a flourishing economy. Williams was the winner of the competition, launched in late 2000, for a new civic centre at Athlone, a modest town in the dead centre of Ireland. The shortlist for the project included a number of outstanding Irish practices, including those of Shay Cleary, McCullough Mulvin, and Grafton Architects – 'I really didn't think we had much of a chance', Williams recalls. 'But on reflection perhaps not being Irish was an advantage. At the interview, I talked of a more European dimension to our thinking and our sense of urbanity'. The civic centre had to accommodate not only a council chamber and local authority offices but also a new public library. Much new building that had taken place in Athlone in recent decades was of mediocre quality, so the civic centre project was seen as an opportunity to put Athlone on the map. The site was in the centre of the town, close to the much rebuilt, but basically medieval, St Mary's church and was created by demolishing the old council offices and some adjacent industrial buildings.

The masterplan instigated by the Irish National Buildings Agency, within which the architects worked, provided for the creation of new public space around the building. Architecturally, a broadly contextual proposal was to be expected. In the event, Williams gave Athlone a building that has no obviously Irish roots. He exploited the potential of the site for a building that could be appreciated in the round but which eschews picturesqueness in favour of incisive composition. Some of the most prominent Irish architectural projects

of recent years – Dublin's Temple Bar is an obvious example – have been conspicuously contextual and driven by the imperative of urban repair. But the International Style has its place in Irish architectural history, seen most notably, perhaps, in the work of Scott Tallon Walker. In Athlone, Williams seized the opportunity to create a frankly modern landmark building, part of a recognisable European tradition, which succeeds in terms of context by means of its appropriate scale and sensitive composition. Indeed, the civic centre, opened in 2004, has the classic white look of the Modern Movement (though the reconstituted stone with which it is clad is actually subtly off-white). Like the Unicorn Theatre, the civic centre is an excellent piece of efficient spatial planning, with more than a touch of expressive drama. The 18-metre-tall, top-lit atrium and principal staircase provides the requisite air of civic pride and is a surprisingly generous gesture in a building totalling just 4200 square metres. The processional stair leads to the imposing double-height council chamber, lit by a central oculus of Kahnian inspiration. The library space too is double height, with offices located above.

Generosity is the keynote of the building, mediating its potentially severe formalism. And, as usual in Williams' work, detailing is precise. The practice designed everything from the public square that fronts the civic centre down to the door handles. For Athlone, the project represents a real infusion of sophisticated modernism, symbolising the ongoing regeneration of the Irish hinterland. Williams' building is a confident and convincing response to the challenge of creating a municipal monument for a new age – not surprisingly it has won 10 major awards.

Williams has recently returned to Athlone to work on two smaller projects. The town's new art gallery occupies a site on the banks of the river Shannon, close to the monumental Catholic church. It combines new-build with the conversion of a former temperance hall, a modest structure but retained for its associations with the temperance campaigner Father Mathew. Williams has also designed an army memorial for the town, to be sited at the base of the walls of the castle.

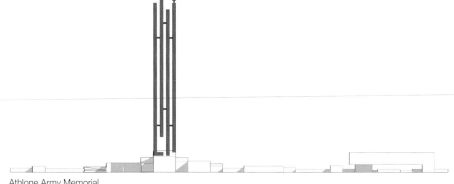

Athlone Army Memorial

The new opera house in Wexford, which opened in time for the October 2008 festival, is the largest of Williams' Irish projects to date. Wexford is one of the major events of the Irish cultural year, comparable to the Glyndebourne or Aldeburgh festivals in Britain and, like them, staged at a remove from the capital city. Like Glyndebourne, the festival made do for many years with a very inadequate venue – the old Theatre Royal was not a distinguished 19th-century building and the facilities it offered audiences and performers were dire. The decision being taken to demolish it and build a new theatre on the same site, the Office of Public Works, a body fundamental to the development scene in Ireland, produced a masterplan for the €33-million project. On the basis both of the Unicorn and his Irish work, Williams was invited to join the team – as a keen operagoer, he relished the opportunity to work on an opera house.

As in the case of the Unicorn, the site was tight, even after a former printing works had been acquired to expand it. Moreover, the decision was taken to retain and convert (they were largely rebuilt in replica) a run of 19th-century terraced houses that concealed the theatre site from the town's high street. Wexford is a small town with small-scale buildings and the new theatre makes a powerful impact viewed from the far side of the river Slaney, with the fly tower an inevitably dominant presence. At close range, it remains a hidden presence, like its predecessor – Williams speaks of the ancillary spaces 'oozing into urban cavities of the surrounding backland plots'. The audience enters through an unassuming set of doors punching out the lower storey in the Victorian terrace. The qualities of the building emerge when you have passed through those doors. As at the Unicorn, the foyer space and auditorium are locked together structurally. The atrium that forms the social focus of the building is a place to gather, to see and be seen, with a series of bars on various levels. But it is the auditorium, formed on the traditional horseshoe pattern, which is the heart of the place. Williams likens it to a cello, a musical instrument in its own right, lined in American walnut. The effect is luxurious without being ostentatious, the kind of restraint seen in Ireland's finest Georgian houses.

The quality of materials and craftsmanship is remarkable but they are orchestrated by Williams' legendary attention to detail. There is a visibly sensual element to his art, a relish for using timber, stone, concrete and other materials in combination to reveal their distinct qualities. Kieran Long, writing in the Architects' Journal, compared the auditorium at Wexford with that at Glyndebourne (designed by Michael Hopkins) and concluded that Wexford was the finer achievement – 'A taut and modelled skin of timber, which distorts and shifts, but is always whole. The steeper lines of the balconies, ending beautifully as they turn toward the stage, are fabulous from every angle.' Long was critical, however, of the theatre's failure to impact on the surrounding townscape. Yet the building's 'backyard' location is a key part of the character of Wexford – the intention was never to create an urban monument. The informality of the place was fundamental to the institution, and this quality has been preserved in its new incarnation. The scale of the building and its contribution to Wexford's urban silhouette only becomes really apparent when it is viewed from the opposite banks of the river Slaney. From there, the new fly tower, auditorium and the upper parts of the building appear as a 'captured pavilion' (Williams' description) in the skyline alongside the spires of Wexford's two Puginian Gothic churches and the Italianate tower of the Franciscan friary, announcing the presence of an exceptional new cultural landmark in the historic townscape.

Wexford Opera House

Wexford Opera House

Williams took enormous pains to understand Wexford and its festival before beginning work on the project. As the designs for the auditorium were being developed, a mock-up of the orchestra pit was constructed in a Dublin warehouse so that the festival's artistic director could provide his expert input. Understanding the client's needs is fundamental to the early stages of any Williams project. Equally, Williams is the first to credit the contribution of his fellow professionals – the architectural team at the office of Public Works, who set the project up, theatre consultants Carr & Angier (Peter Angier describes the new auditorium as one of the great small opera houses of the world) and Arup Acoustics were all indispensable members of the team for Wexford. After eight years working in the country, it is hard to imagine that Williams will not find further commissions in Ireland. He feels that he has, in turn, learned from Ireland, not least from the enthusiasm and drive of his clients there. The project's success certainly underlines Williams' position as one of the most accomplished designers of performing arts buildings globally.

The imperative to respect context was equally to the fore with the Long House, a project Williams designed for a private client in the affluent St John's Wood quarter of London. The budget was generous (and remains confidential) but the site – in a conservation area and surrounded by existing buildings – was tight and particularly problematic. The brief was demanding – the client wanted a large house to cater for the needs of a family with young children, but with spaces for formal entertaining too. The big garden, which was such a key asset of the site, had to be preserved. The triangular plan, reflecting the disjunction of two city grids, allows the house to fill the available land, and to open up to the garden. From the modest mews, which provides the street approach to the house, there are few clues as to its internal character. The 49-metre-long street elevation consists

mostly of a solid wall of London stock brick that fronts a long, single-storey family wing. There is an impressive swimming pool at basement level, with a trabeated concrete structure forming the roof, a favourite device of Williams, used at the Unicorn and Athlone. Here, however, with top light streaming down one wall, it gives the sense of a truly subterranean space with a great weight above it. Beyond is the two-storey block, clad in white render, which contains an impressive sequence of double-height entrance hall, dining room and living room, with a large kitchen tucked away behind. Family bedrooms are upstairs, with accommodation for guests and staff located over the garage that terminates the block. Even by Williams' high standards, this is a virtuoso exercise in compact planning – clarity of plan is one of the planks of Williams' design credo. He aims for 'a celebratory way of moving through buildings' and stresses the importance of 'the way light comes into a building and the way views out are handled'.

The Long House reflects these aims. Necessarily horizontal in emphasis, it breaks out into double-height space, using extensive glazing, where needed, to capitalise on garden views. Internally, materials include oak flooring, limestone and white plaster, providing a neutral backcloth for furniture and works of art. The house can only be properly enjoyed by the privileged few allowed to penetrate beyond its (somewhat enigmatic) front door, but in urban terms it makes a positive if discreet addition to an area of London where the scope for innovative new design seems extremely limited. Williams' client has written of the house in glowing terms as 'a joy to live in', providing 'a logical integration between the rooms and the way we wanted to live'. As an instance of modern architecture working successfully in the traditional city, the project might be compared, for example, with Erno Goldfinger's famous terrace of houses at Willow Road, Hampstead.

With some relatively large, and certainly critically well-regarded, projects completed, Williams could be seen, in mid-career, as poised for the really big job that affirms his position among the front rank of European architects. The intense urbanism of his work might seem a very English quality. He is certainly adept at working in classic heritage locations, but it would be too easy to underestimate the international influences that form his work and shape his thinking.

Alongside the Canterbury theatre, there is the project, won in competition in 2007, for a new district museum in Chichester. The site is 200 metres from the medieval cathedral, fronting on to an ancient street but in a part of the city somewhat fractured by post-war development (including a destructive relief road), and is currently used for car parking. It contains the remains, however, discovered in the 1970s, of the city's Roman baths, which are to be incorporated into the museum development. The museum building, which defers to the scale of the historic street, is to be clad in reconstituted stone, a material used by Williams at Athlone. In Chichester, a number of major religious and secular buildings are constructed of pale limestone – Williams' choice of material for this new civic building provides a clear continuum. Externally, a turret-like form has been added asymmetrically, rising significantly above the established street line and symbolising the civic significance of the building. A rooftop panoramic window provides fine views of the cathedral and city. Inside, another of the architect's processional stairs connects the galleries accommodating the permanent collections and temporary exhibitions. The plan is typically clear and highly practical. Williams has also designed an associated residential development to complete the urban block on which the museum will be located. This will be fronted in local brick as a deliberate foil to the adjacent museum – a very deliberate balance of materials – with the two street façades meeting on a strongly articulated corner. The museum will be constructed in advance of the residential scheme, the site of which will become a temporary garden.

Williams' scheme for the new museum in Mosegård, Denmark was placed second in the 2005 invited international competition – his was the only British practice to be asked to submit. Fated to remain unbuilt, this was one of Williams' most sophisticated projects, taking a confident but considered approach to the spectacular hilltop site and offering the prospect of magnificent interiors distinguished by the expert use of natural light. Nordic countries have figured strongly on the competition map for Williams – witness his schemes for the Kulturhus (library, art gallery and theatre) in Flekkefijord, Norway, the Maritime Museum at Helsingør, Denmark, and the theatre and "Jazzhouse" in the small Norwegian town of Molde (2007), once again an exercise in contextual modernism. In Germany, there have been projects for the Friedrich Nietzsche Archive at Naumburg and the Modern Literature Museum in Marbach am Neckar (extending the existing 19th-century Schiller Museum) as well as for a new university library in Darmstadt.

Perhaps the most challenging German project with which Williams has been involved was his competition entry for the proposed Nazi Dokumentszentrum in Munich. The centre will provide a harrowing record, using film, photography and written records, of the atrocities of the Nazi regime – this in a city where Nazism was born. Located close to Paul Troost's HQ Building for Hitler, the Fuhrerbau (now used as an arts and music building for the university), where the infamous 1938 Munich Agreement was signed, the centre is intended to be anything but celebratory. Competing again against a distinguished rollcall of international stars (including Moshe Safdie, Peter Eisenman, Kengo Kuma and Wandel Hoefer Lorch – the latter responsible for a striking new synagogue in Munich) Williams proposes a stone-clad building in which any hint of monumentality on the exterior is dispelled by an informal disposition of masses. Inside, there is a large underground gallery with an impressive stair providing a connection to the upper levels. An asymmetric disposition of glazing helps to further reduce any element of monumentality and connects the interior spaces with key vistas into the city and the remaining physical fragments of the Nazi hegemony – a key element in the competition brief.

In recessionary times, Williams may not regret too much his lack of involvement with the world of commercial and speculative residential development. His belief that good buildings come out of a close relationship with the client/user might seem to be at odds with the commercial agenda. Yet Williams is an architect intent on building – he believes in creating projects with 'a core simplicity that can weather the planning process'. Quite recently, he has been working on a proposal for a 24-storey, 65-metre-high residential tower close to the Thames at Vauxhall, South London. In contrast to many London riverside sites, the context is highly constrained (by roads and a railway viaduct) – and located within a protected view corridor. The result is a highly complex exercise in modelling. One of Williams' key concerns is to achieve a satisfactory relationship between the base of the tower, the skyline and the street, to design a building that has street presence while rising to become a pinnacle at its summit.

It is typical of Keith Williams, when confronting a building type new to his practice, to revert to fundamental principles and examine the key issue of the dialogue between the building and the city. Williams' architecture is firmly modern, rooted in modernist aesthetics with their roots in the early 20th century. But his sensibility is very much that of the 21st century. He aims to create buildings with a long life, hardwearing and adaptable and sustainable in the fullest sense of the term. With their strong sense of place, identity and history, Williams' buildings are good neighbours, a status they achieve not through deference or timidity but through their confidence and dignity and the way in which they complement a wide variety of established contexts. They form a remarkable portfolio for an architect with many years of work ahead of him.

The next decade of work from Williams' studio is eagerly awaited.

Kenneth Powell is an architectural historian and critic based in London. He is an Honorary Fellow of the RIBA and the author of many books, including New London Architecture 2 *and* Richard Rogers: Complete Works.

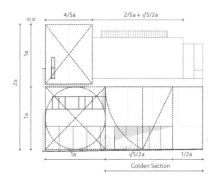

Chichester District Museum

In Conversation with Keith Williams
by Dr Sandra O'Connell

Our initial conversation takes place in Keith Williams' studio in a former warehouse in Holborn. The 'shop windows', where models are stored rather than displayed, offer a first glimpse into the activities of the practice. Inside, the office is spacious and open-plan, illuminated on this dark winter day by tall windows and roof-lights. The office is very international and the atmosphere busy but informal. The firm moved to Holborn five years ago from Covent Garden, attracted by lower rents, generous office space and the eclectic atmosphere. 'The area is very diverse', Keith explains, 'you find design studios and nearby legal practices and the Inns of Court, and there's even an undertaker a few streets up'. Our conversation begins as we move through the office, looking at models, architectural awards, large photographs of completed schemes and sketches of current work.

Sandra O'Connell: Your book is called *Architecture of the Specific*. Why have you chosen this title?

Keith Williams: I suppose there is a specific quality to the work that we do. That everything is considered. Most of our buildings are a precise response to client ambition, to the brief and the context. Each move is very carefully and deliberately considered. It seems an appropriate term. There is 'specificity' in what we do.

SC: Your practice covers a diverse range of building types from theatres, museums and an opera house to a one-off house and you are currently working on a residential tower on Black Prince Road on London's South Bank. Is there a thread that runs through all of these projects, perhaps themes like light, space, form, scale and materiality?

KRW: You are right to pick on those themes; they do seem to be, to a degree, recurrent. I think it's good to have a diversity of projects, intellectually as well as in a straightforward business sense. These themes are part of the conceptual glue that give a common thread to much of what we do across our differing projects. First you tackle the problem of designing a very low horizontal house, as in the case of The Long House, and then you face the complexity of how to make a tall building that has this series of floor plates, which give it stratification. For example, if you

were to clad a tall building in glass and then light it at night internally, it will appear as a series of plates. You will have a tall building with a horizontal grain to it. We chose, however, not to do that. Instead, we wanted to make a solid building that has a series of slots cut into it, which accentuates the verticality. We also tapered the building; it is wider at its base than it is at its sides. We would not have necessarily thought of this when we started the commission, this is more of an evolution. The tapering of the tower flowed from the constraints of daylight and sunlight falling on the adjacent neighbouring properties as a result of a tower.

The plan is trapezoidal and we needed to find a three-dimensional form of expression. We came up with the concept of two hands embracing and clasping the tower's inner core that gives this tall building its unusual form. It has given us the opportunity to think afresh and create diversity in the office.

Intellectual diversity therefore flows from project diversity, in that it allows you to create from certain issues. In a way, the best architecture does come from difficult constraints. The worst brief you could have is a big open site, a client saying 'I don't mind what you design', and an open budget. Somehow greater creativity comes from constraints. Take Ireland, it produced some of the most extraordinary literature often from very difficult circumstances.

SC: Your projects tend to be for complex urban sites where consideration has to be paid to issues such as neighbouring properties and urban context. One of your most difficult projects to date must have been the Wexford Opera House in Ireland, located in a highly constricted backstreet site context. It must have been difficult to fit the complex programme of an opera house into these constrains?

KRW: Very much so but when you have the chance to do an opera house, you take it. We did this project in collaboration with the Office of Public Works in Ireland and a significant amount of groundwork had already been done. But collectively we took the project in a new and fresh direction. We have become quite good at stacking volumes and making connections between them. At Wexford the main 780-seat auditorium and stage are approximately at ground level, whereas the second auditorium is at least a level below and other functions are stacked above. However, we still managed to create a four-storey, top-lit atrium space and to thread through the whole complex a processional stair, a device we use in many of our buildings.

SC: Sometimes you are not only mastering these constraints but you seem to enjoy playing with them and turning them on their head. You said before that there is a kind of perversity in your work and that you enjoy mass and solidity.

KRW: I talked elsewhere of trying to establish a set of ground rules. Yes, I do enjoy solidity in architecture. Take for example the Long House and its subterranean swimming pool. It has a sense of a labyrinth, even though light is flooding down one side. The house feels of the earth and that solidity is very important to me. I enjoy solid mass and it creates the opportunity to incise and bring light into a building in unexpected ways. This is probably true of some of the grandest and the simplest buildings, such as the Pantheon in Rome with its oculus. It is incredibly simple but the way the light comes into the building changes according to the weather and the time of the day and the seasons. In a way if you get simple ground rules right, the light does the rest for you. It creates that luminosity, with which the human soul engages in a fundamental way.

SC: Are your clients conscious of the effect of light in your buildings? I am thinking here for example of the Athlone Civic Offices and how the council chamber is bathed and transformed by natural light.

KRW: Maybe you need to put that to them. I suppose after a while when you work in an environment these things become more familiar and accepted. But certainly when people began using the building for the first time and had a sense of the light coming into the council chamber, there was something quite ceremonial about it. And there is a certain ritual and ceremony associated with council meetings, even though they sometimes have to deal with quite mundane issues.

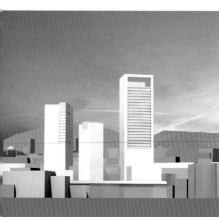

Bergamo Civic Centre

SC: In other buildings, I'm thinking here of theatres and museums, daylight is not always wanted, because it needs to be controlled. How does this affect your design?

KRW: We had a long debate on the Chichester Museum, where we felt quite strongly that daylight was a positive element for the permanent galleries. But we have been persuaded in the end that this particular gallery cannot operate with daylight, because of the nature of the artefacts, which are quite small scale and require specific display. Therefore, in this building the light comes in at street level, so there is a large vitrine that runs along the length of the museum. Accent light is then brought in through roof lights, discreetly placed, until at the top of the promenade stairs sequence there is, what I term, the 'cathedral window', a viewing point that gives views of the Chichester Cathedral. This area is highly glazed and flooded with light. The idea was also used at Wexford, where at the end of the long ascent, light begins to be introduced from above, and a huge viewing window offers views over the Slaney estuary. So it's a kind of reward.

SC: This device also allows you to reconnect to the urban context. Sometimes these buildings can feel like labyrinths. How important is the urban context to your buildings?

KRW: I suppose most of our projects are urban – the nearest to a greenfield site was the competition for the Moesgård Ethnography Museum in Åarhus, Denmark where we created this 'acropolis' museum complex on the brow of a hill. And there the context was making an obvious visual connection with an existing 18th-century manor house. But from that point views were also available over the sea and forest, so the landscape and vista was also the context there. Even in a situation where there is very little obvious built context, we try and make these contextual connections. In most other projects we have built within a town or a city, so there is more context and complexity that comes to bear on the project. Increasingly we are working on larger urban buildings, having cut our teeth on smaller civic projects.

SC: You seem to take a cue from the urban environment but you don't seem to make a very literal response to it. I am thinking for example of the competition for a cultural centre in Flekkefjord, Norway where a cue came from the horizontal grain of the surrounding timber houses but you have immediately turned this on its head.

KRW: I have never seen any point in building 'in keeping', which is what many people might view as appropriate. What they mean is that when you live in a Georgian city you make some kind of a fake Georgian architecture. I am great admirer of Georgian architecture but I can't see any point of drawing a line in the sand and refusing to believe that there is valid cultural contribution from the future. Somehow then we cease to experiment and create and I can't see any point in being an architect if you do that. We feel that it is important to make a new building that is clearly of its age or maybe even ahead of its time; a building that can either through its colour, material quality, or its scale, or the way it opens itself up to allow people to look in, have a relationship with the physical circumstances in which it is situated.

But there is also the perversity on which we touched earlier, for example in the Unicorn, where we eroded the base of the tower and made a very heavy staircase appear to float. For the Flekkefjord competition in Norway we made a play on the horizontal timber boarding that characterises many buildings in the town but in our building we used white glass and laid it out vertically. I think this says, 'on the one hand we are part of you but we are not trying to be exactly like you'. This is a special building, it's a cultural focus, it can afford to step out of the convention and make a statement.

The same applies to the new Marlowe Theatre in Canterbury. The re-clad flytower will respond in scale to the spire of Canterbury Cathedral; it tapers pinnacle-like but is re-sculpted and reordered. It will be the second highest point in the city and clad in stainless steel mesh. Copper is used to clad the elevated second auditorium, which recalls both the dark hue of the city's roof tiles and the prevailing brick in the town without mimicking it.

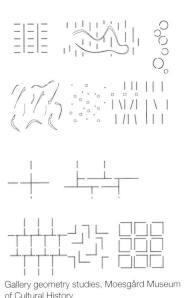

Gallery geometry studies, Moesgård Museum of Cultural History

SC: Do you consider yourself fortunate to have been able to design such important cultural buildings?

KRW: Very much so. When you are in architecture college and are making a list of the projects that you would eventually like to design – I have designed quite a number of them.

SC: How did you find returning to the small scale of the one-off house after designing large theatres and civic projects?

KRW: We were actually working on the Long House in London at the same time as Athlone and the Unicorn were on site. In many ways, the Long House was a more demanding project as the clients, who have become good friends, were living just up the road from us, so there was really no escape. I remember when the builder promised that the house was complete, I went there with the client who called me out at 6.45am on a Saturday morning, only to discover a leak in the pool.

SC: It must have been also very satisfying designing a house and seeing the difference a good design can make in people's lives?

KRW: Yes it was, but it was equally satisfying seeing the Unicorn Theatre fill for the first time. Lord Attenborough came down to open it and the great and the good from the theatre world were there. The place was filled with children and there was a fantastic buzz. It was similarly rewarding when the Wexford Opera House opened. I had placed myself strategically in the auditorium so I could watch the audience arriving on the first night and it was incredible seeing all these open mouths.

SC: Nothing could have prepared the audience at Wexford for this experience as the modest entrance offers no clue about the grand scale of the auditorium inside.

KRW: When you can shock, surprise and delight people with architecture, this has got to be a good outcome; seeing something that they had not thought to be possible.

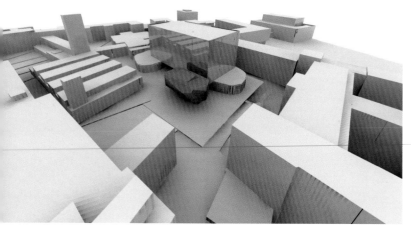

Universitäts und Landesbibliothek TU Darmstadt

At lunchtime our conversation moves to the recently refurbished Royal Festival Hall in the South Bank Centre. The restaurant – themed on the Skylon structure that once occupied the adjacent Festival site – offers a magnificent panorama of London's skyline with tall windows looking out over the Thames. In our view is Embankment Place, a large office building above Charing Cross Station on which Keith worked as a young architect with Terry Farrell. It takes our conversation back to Keith's training as an architect and his first years in practice.

SC: What made you choose architecture as your profession?

KRW: I always had a fascination for buildings and how they are put together. I remember as a child being completely mesmerised by how the Millbank tower was lit up emerald green at night – it was a truly heroic building. I was equally fascinated by the roof of Waterloo Station and wanted to know how it was put together. I also had an interest in drawing and sketching and was good at maths, so architecture was an ideal option.

SC: After graduating from Kingston and Greenwich, did you have any desire to gain work experience abroad?

KRW: I would have liked to go to Australia but I did not manage it. I graduated in the middle of a recession but found work first with Sheppard Robson and then, as you know, with Farrell. We were very concerned with urbanism and public space and I also learned a lot on engineering and how things are put together.

SC: What was the most memorable building you designed during this time?

KRW: I was project architect for the Henley Regatta Headquarters (1986), which became quite a well-regarded building. I also worked on Embankment Place, the redevelopment sitting above Charing Cross Station. It's a highly contextual building and belongs to the great tradition of riverside pavilions. I remember that in order to show the building in its context, fifteen of us produced a 10-metre-long drawing of the entire riverside, each producing a bit of the river elevation, which we then stuck together. We made the argument that, although this is a big building, in terms of the river scale it is actually quite appropriate.

SC: In 1987, you set up your first practice Pawson Williams Architects. What motivated you – were you a bad employee or had you always wanted to work for yourself?

KRW: Was I a bad employee? Maybe, I don't know, but I do know that I worked damn hard. I think I always wanted to set up on my own. Even when I worked with Farrell, I worked on a freelance basis. It was a difficult time to set up practice, at the start of a recession. Our first built project was an exhibition for the Natural History Museum and we managed to get through the recession with work like this. Eventually, I wanted to break away from the constraints of a partnership and set up Keith Williams Architects. I have a very creative relationship with my co-director Richard, who has been with the practice from the start.

SC: How do you approach a new design, does the white page hold a terror for you?

KRW: Of course, but I enjoy getting under the skin of the project to try and understand the client's concerns and motivations. Often there is an undercurrent to a project and you need to understand what the true project is. Or you get a project where brief and budget don't

match; you need to work out how you can deliver the client's ambitions within these opposing parameters.

SC: How do you develop a design and how important are sketches and models?

KRW: Design to me has always been a nonlinear process, even though the constraints of programme, project timetable and delivery say that you start at stage A and develop to the next stage. In a way it forces the pace and decision-making and it's a convenient further constraint as you don't have an infinite amount of time to make decisions. But I feel we haven't really tested projects unless we have explored them through a number of different methods and media.

Many projects start in my sketchbook and get developed from there. It allows me to tackle spatial relationships or formal junctions and I feed this back to the studio. But we really test buildings through models. Some are specially made but that comes after slightly scruffy and wonky models, pieces of card stuck together, which are not there to be admired. The scale can be 1:1 but more usually it is 1:50 or 1:20, we make them when we explore more precise spatial arrangements but they can also be conceptual and very small. To develop the stone brise soleil for Athlone Civic Offices, we made a 1:1 prototype with the engineers Buro Happold. In the process we learned that by shaving away the underside of the mock-up, we were able to bring diffused light into the building, whilst also cutting out solar gain. In the Athlone project we were also fortunate enough to have the license to design a suite of ironmongery and outdoor furniture such as the benches. I have also recently designed some chairs, which I am in the process of patenting. But trying to launch a new furniture range in the middle of a recession is probably not a good idea. In each case you try and design something as elegant and functional as it can be.

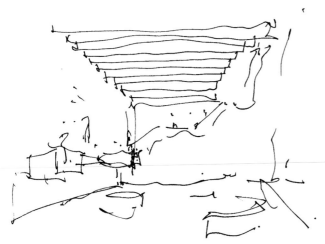

Chichester District Museum

SC: Is the desire to design all aspects of the building, down to the door handles, partly a control thing? And how do you feel when you revisit your buildings?

KRW: Yes, all architects are control freaks but I think we have to accept that buildings change and a good building should be capable of change. Perhaps though the buildings my practice is designing – the Architecture of the Specific – are not as loose fit as others. They are quite specific in their purpose.

SC: A lot of your work – theatres, opera houses and museums – seems to focus on the arts. Are you being labelled as an architect for cultural buildings?

KRW: We would be ok with that. Culture is a great measure of civilisation. Culture is not something you have to do to survive but need to do in order to have a civilised society. I always consider them first and foremost public buildings, they are a measure of how good you are as an architect. You are judged on this by the public too.

SC: You have been invited to participate in a number of northern European competitions, including for the Flekkefjord cultural centre and Moesgård Museum in Åarhus, Denmark. Do you think that your work strikes a cord with a Scandinavian design sensibility?

KRW: To a degree our work is influenced by Arne Jacobsen, for example I admire the SAS hotel in Copenhagen or his town hall in Åarhus. There are aspects of what we do that have been informed by Jacobsen. I think there is also a clarity in what we do. We aim for a simplistic elegance.

SC: When the Athlone Civic Offices came up for publication in *Architecture Ireland* (the journal of the RIAI), the editorial board was initially astounded that this building was actually in Ireland. The contemporary clean lines, crisp white stone and unashamed monumentality shown in the photographs seemed to belong to a European Modern.

KRW: I have always considered Athlone as a European building. I believe that Ireland sees itself very much part of Europe and the building epitomises these strong links.

Athlone Civic Centre

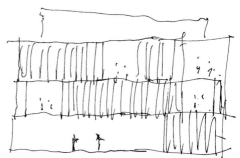

NS-Dokumentationszentrum

SC: You also have some very complex projects on the drawing board at the moment, for example the invited competition for a centre in Munich that documents the history of the Nazi party. This must be a difficult commission and a difficult building to design? Is it a kind of museum?

KRW: The title of the project is NS-Dokumentationszentrum and a small number of these centres have been built in other locations in Germany. It is easy to interpret it as a museum, but certainly the organisers of the competition don't see it like that. They see it literally as a 'documentation centre'. It is not intended to have artefacts from the Nazi era but it is intended to have documents, magazines and newsreels. It's a place for analysis to understand, perhaps, how such things come to pass. What's interesting is that they come to pass in times of very difficult and extreme financial circumstances; rather more extreme than what we are currently experiencing. Countries where you have a completely collapsing economy, as Germany was in the 1930s, can produce extreme politics. You have extreme politics in Zimbabwe with the collapsing economy; a different type, but extreme.

It is such a charged subject and the team who worked on the competition in my office included several young Germans because I was interested in how they see the whole subject. However, it is difficult and the subject is so complex, so delicate. How do you make a building that has anything to do with that extraordinarily evil period – because it must not be celebratory, it must not be monumentalised. It needs to be neutral yet purposeful. So what we are trying to do is to make a building that has an elegance and a modesty; that has a sense of spaciousness without grandeur; a building that is despite its relative large scale very modest and quite deliberately very asymmetrical and abstract, which relates back to an art and architecture that would have been unlikely to find favour with the Nazi regime. So maybe that's the best we can do. It is incredibly complex politically because in the building next to the site the Munich Agreement of 1938 was signed.

It is very strange walking around the building, although it's currently a university building, thinking that from this building world history changed, and from the building grew a movement which, less than a decade later, had caused Europe to lay in ruins with 50 million people dead. So this is scary stuff.

SC: Are these the kind of challenges that keep you motivated and what projects would you still like to do?

KRW: It is interesting that when this competition happened, it hadn't really occurred to me that this kind of project would come up. And this is what keeps architecture interesting. You never know what the next project is. But I think I would like to do a pure concert hall. I have also become interested in building tall, having started with a 24-storey tower. It would be interesting to see what we would do if we had a tall building without any height constraints. The question is how would you build in the Middle East? But we are also doing quite modest work, including a war memorial in Athlone. And it would be fun to design an opera set.

SC: You win a lot of your work through invited competitions. How important are competitions to the practice? Are they important to pushing out new boundaries in design terms?

KRW: I suppose competitions are mixed blessings. On the one hand, they are important to get projects and they create opportunities for fresh examination and thinking. We found they are often used as a test bed of ideas. The stone louvres you find on the façade of Athlone were first developed during a competition for a university project which we did not win, and then applied on a much larger scale for the Centro Culturale in Turin, which we also did not win, until finally we got to build them in Athlone. Like most firms, we lose more than we win. Competitions are an important part of the development of architecture. But they need to be real. I think it is very important that when clients are going through this process that they are fairly confident they can build this thing and that they understand how much cost and investment goes into it. Clients need to make sure that they have a clear and coherent strategy behind it and that they know how to choose a scheme and have architectural expertise on the selection panel.

SC: Where do you find new creative ideas?

KRW: One of the advantages of living in a capital city like London is that there is usually a good exhibition on, or an interesting building to see. Before Christmas I went to see the Francis Bacon exhibition at the Tate. A lot of these things are really subliminal. You don't quite necessarily change what you are doing but it is interesting to remind yourself what these paintings contain; there is an architectural quality to some of the Bacon paintings, there is usually a sense of structure. I found all of that very valuable. Also the opera sets by Alison Chitty for *The Minotaur*, which were incredibly strident and powerful but also very simple. I find it stimulating to visit as many places as I can. I am just back from Hong Kong and was very excited but also taken aback by some of the new buildings there. It has been 12 years since I last visited. Travelling causes you to re-evaluate what you are doing.

SC: You also have a very international and young office. How important is your staff in bringing in fresh ideas?

KRW: Very important and they bring in a lot skills. And while we may have Germans and Norwegians, it turns out that they have worked in Australia or lived in Argentina. I think we have quite a nomadic lot, which means that the knowledge depth is quite significant. There is usually someone who will say, 'Ah yes, there is this small building in Uruguay that is a bit like that'. Nothing is wholly new it seems.

Dr Sandra Andrea O'Connell is editor of Architecture Ireland, *the official journal of the Royal Institute of the Architects of Ireland. She writes regularly on architecture, contributes to panel discussions and is Curator of the annual Open House Dublin weekend, Ireland's largest architectural event. Sandra holds a PhD in English Literature from Trinity College Dublin and regularly contributes criticism on Irish and European Modernism to conferences and academic publications. A collection of essays on the Irish–Russian poet George Reavey (1907–1976) edited by Sandra O'Connell is due to appear with Lilliput Press Dublin in 2010.*

Centro Culturali di Torino

Selected Projects

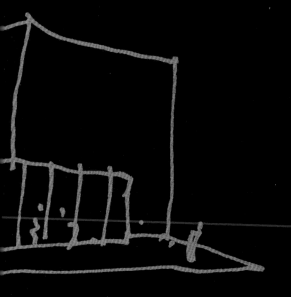

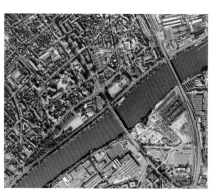

Centre Régional de la Musique et de la Voix (CRMV)
Argenteuil, France

Argenteuil is one of Paris's most populous suburbs and is situated on the River Seine some 12 kilometres northwest of the city centre in the Département du Val d'Oise. Dating from the 7th century, the suburb expanded significantly with the arrival of the railway in the 19th century and was subsequently made famous through its association with the arts, particularly the paintings of the impressionist Claude Monet and as the birthplace of Georges Braque.

The Centre Régional de la Musique et de la Voix (CRMV) was a key element in the local council's urban regeneration strategy for a large vacant tract of land alongside the Seine at the town's arrival point across the bridge from Paris. Occupying a key site close by the approach to the Pont d'Argenteuil, the 13,500-square-metre CRMV was one of Williams' earliest cultural projects and was joint winner in the invited international competition. The building was intended to house a regional music college, a triple-theatre complex including auditoria of 900 and 300 seats, as well as a multipurpose flat-floor hall and a médiatheque.

The CRMV project was organised such that its public façade addressed a new public square separating the building from the foot of the bridge. The main foyer rises the full height of the building and contains the principal elements of public circulation that unite all levels and elements within the building complex.

The set of four columns and canopy establishes an heroic order to the composition while also allowing freer-flowing forms within its volume to introduce more expressive elements encapsulated within the formality of the main architectural order.

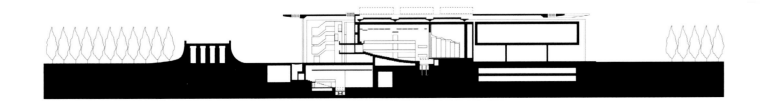

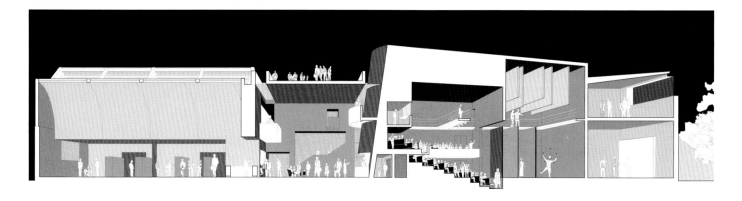

The MERCAT Centre
Dingwall, Scotland

Dingwall is a small market town located 19 kilometres north of Inverness, in Ross and Cromarty, on the eastern coast of the Highlands of Scotland. It was an important Viking centre and became a Royal Burgh in the 13th century. Remnants of the medieval plan remain in the modern town, while its edges, once arable land, are now largely open plots and parking areas shaped by its role as a livestock market.

The 2600-square-metre MERCAT Centre for the Highland Council, an early arts project for the office, was an ambitious plan intended as the flagship project in an arts-led urban regeneration initiative designed to inject important new cultural activity into the town and surrounding region.

The siting of the MERCAT allowed Williams to propose a new reinforced edge to the town. Using the design of the building to set up a dense façade to the town's skirting road, he opened up the centre's face toward the town, where the main, triple-height entrance hall sits axially from the Mercat cross outside the town's ancient stone Town House.

Bringing visual, performing and literary arts together under one roof, the MERCAT Centre encompassed a regional library, a 200-seat flexible format theatre and cinema, as well as an art gallery and additional spaces for artists-in-residence and teaching studios. Although the project remains unexecuted, the Centre was intended to link with the unique Fèis Rois arts program, which celebrates and teaches Gaelic music traditions, and provide a renewed cultural focus for the local and regional community.

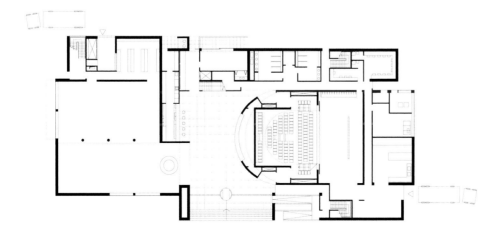

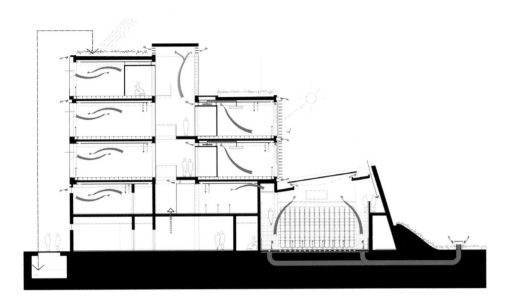

Centre for Business Management and Postgraduate Studies, Anglia Ruskin University
Chelmsford, England, 2000

The earliest of a number of key university projects, the invited project for the new 4950-square-metre Centre for Business Management and Postgraduate Studies was based around an internal layout with a governing proposition of adaptability. It proved a critical test bed for ideas, notably the practice's approach to fully integrated, low-energy architectural design, including the use of pre-cast louvres, which were later realised in Athlone Civic Centre, 2001–2004.

The overall composition is in essence a simple tripartite, horizontally composed, linear five-storey block. The base of the building comprises a two-storey volume into which all reception and public levels are slotted. These include the principal social spaces, mezzanines, certain specialist teaching and administrative areas as well as the main lecture theatre. The lecture theatre is contained in a skewed, slanted wrap wall that gives this key space a distinctive and memorable form as it slews into the double-height reception hall adjacent to the main entrance.

The next two levels contain primary academic teaching and study spaces organised on either side of a central light trench that draws daylight deep into the heart of the building. Finally, the top level of the building comprises a single-loaded bar containing academic spaces, which surmounts the main teaching levels to the north of the central light trench.

The core at the western end is expressed as a tower punctuating the composition with an architectural full stop, signing the building from a distance. The general scale of the building was intended to balance the existing, adjacent Queens and Sawyer buildings and continue particular uniting elevational features such as the double-storey, colonnaded glazed band alongside the River Chelmer.

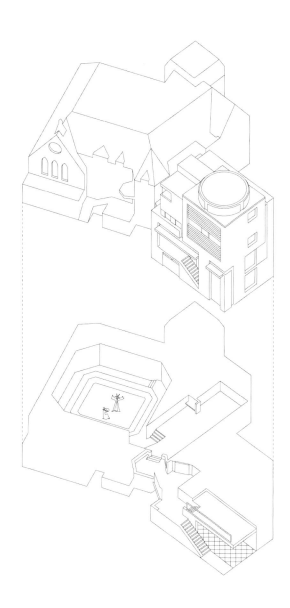

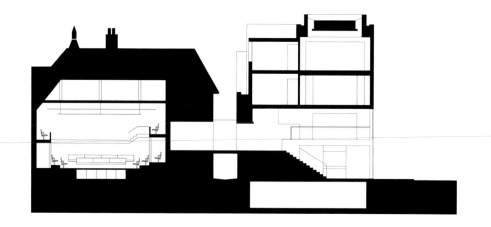

Orange Tree Theatre, Entrance and Rehearsal Building
Richmond, England

The Entrance and Rehearsal Building was the first of two alternative projects on the same site carried out by Keith Williams for the Orange Tree Theatre in Richmond between 1997 and 2004. Although this first project was not ultimately executed, it nevertheless provided a test bed for ideas such as the oculus and the brise soleil, both of which would be achieved in Athlone Civic Centre, several years later.

The Orange Tree Theatre is located on the edge of the Richmond town centre and occupies a 19th-century converted school building in Clarence Street, a side road off the main high street, Kew Road. Founded in 1971, it has become a highly respected 'off West End' theatre presenting new plays, rediscoveries and foreign works. Notably, the theatre has been dubbed 'a pocket sized National Theatre' by critic Michael Billington. The converted Clarence Street building contains a 172-seat theatre-in-the-round, stage management, foyer/bar, dressing rooms and limited other facilities.

Williams' first project involved the design of a new entrance building with rehearsal and design studios above on the site of 47 Kew Road, a very prominent corner junction between Kew Road and Clarence Street, separated from the Orange Tree Theatre by a service alleyway. Number 47 terminates the vista down Kew Road from the town centre and faces onto a triangular public space in front of the Orange Tree public house, the birthplace of the theatre.

Williams re-sited the main entrance for the theatre complex within the new project to face the public space, the Orange Tree public house and the Richmond town centre. The ground and first floors contain the public facilities, including the theatre box office, bar, foyer and exhibition spaces. The alleyway that separates the two buildings is bridged at first floor level, connecting the new foyer to the Clarence Street auditorium.

The mass of the new building was composed to relate directly to its immediate neighbouring buildings and to provide articulation to the skyline and façades. The stage management and rehearsal spaces are contained within an eroded tower form with a raised rooftop circular oculus over the rehearsal area. The corner tower takes its scale from the Orange Tree pub. Williams' design forms a sense of spatial containment to the public open space in front of the site, which for the first time allows the theatre the opportunity to be visible from the town centre. The building design is geometric and abstract in composition, but elements such as the base beneath the main stair and the setback above the bridge link take their scale from horizontal features of the Clarence Street theatre building, ensuring an appropriateness of contextual scale in a mature town centre environment.

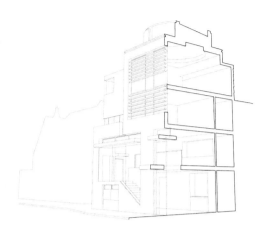

Orange Tree Theatre
Rehearsal Building
Richmond, England, 2002–2003

Williams' second project, and the design that was eventually realised, involved the retention and remodelling of 47 Kew Road to create simple, additional backstage facilities. The combination of the brief and site created a certain paradox – the Orange Tree's most prominently sited building was to house primarily backstage facilities usually out of sight of its audience. However, in this apparent paradox lay the opportunity.

Internally, the remodelled building has created new space for rehearsal, wardrobe, design studio, theatrical workshop and storage space. Williams used the opportunity to step beyond the project's simple internal program and create a striking landmark; the remodelled building acts as a form of billboard, signalling the presence of the Orange Tree Theatre in the townscape.

In urban terms, the remodelled Rehearsal Building (47 Kew Road) and the Orange Tree pub opposite form a pair of unequal gateway buildings of very different architectural styles marking the emergence of Clarence Street onto Kew Road. The existing building's parapets were raised in height and sculpted to achieve an interlocking of form to aid the architectural articulation of the corner building. To establish a contextual link, the broad colour palette of the red brick and pale cream of the stone from the Orange Tree pub was lifted and deployed across the rendered surfaces of the remodelled building to reinforce its new form and detail.

At street level, the building surfaces become a large illuminated poster site allowing current and future shows to be publicised. The remodelled building is contextually derived yet also makes a simple, bold statement of powerful painterly planes and surface composition. The project has re-ordered a mundane building on an important site and announced the Orange Tree's physical presence far more directly, consequently making a significant contribution to the town's mature urban scene.

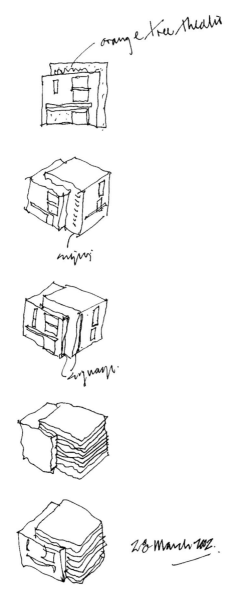

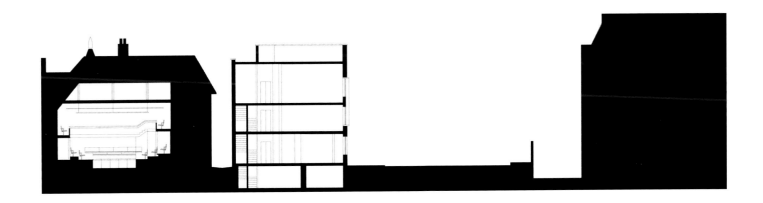

Centro Culturale di Torino
Torino, Italy, 2001

Keith Williams' premiated project for a major arts complex in the Italian city of Torino was the only entry from the UK selected into the final round of this major international competition. The 40,000-square-metre project housed the new city library and a 1200-seat concert hall.

Turin is a city enveloped on three sides by the distant Alps. Its key buildings include secular and religious architecture alongside a large number of individual, private palazzi. The Centro Culturale project was located in the former industrial quarter on the site of the defunct Nebiolo Company fabrication plant. The project was developed not as a single building but as a new, united complex with the library and concert hall at its heart. The internal planning and interconnections allow the grouping to function as if contained within a single building envelope yet are distinguished by the identities of each separate element.

The Library Cube operates at several levels, functioning not only as a major-scale city library and arts complex but also fulfilling a wider urban role. Rising up through its atrium, a grand public stair connects the new street-level forecourt to a public piazza at the top of the building. The rooftop garden piazza was designed to become a new destination point for the city, providing Turin with a totally new type of urban space – largely unique in world cities – granting spectacular views over the city and the Alps.

The vast, vertical atrium is intended as the prime conduit for people accessing the rooftop piazza and those moving within the secure library circulation system to access the various library levels. The library floor levels are laid out before the visitor as a physical expression of layers of knowledge, all instantly visible and recognisable from the entrance point.

The Library Cube, the architectural centrepiece, is seen as a contemporary reinterpretation of the Torinese Renaissance palazzo form, but a palazzo dedicated to information accessible by all citizens, acknowledging the common ownership of knowledge and culture. This idea is embodied in the transparent expression of the public façade of the building, which through its materiality and interplay of natural and artificial light is designed to appear as a glowing crystalline form.

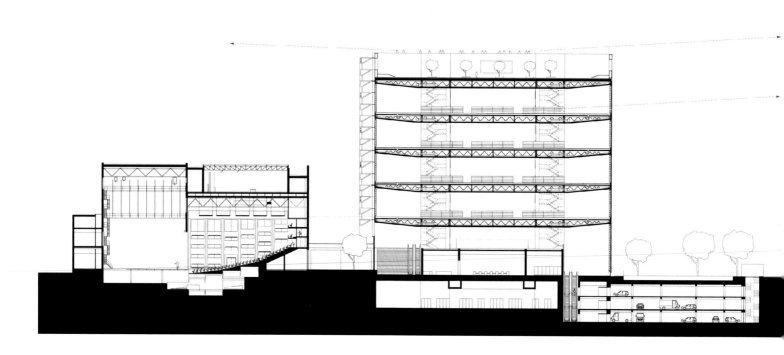

The 1200-seat concert hall is set back within the plan arrangement and separated from the main library tower and atrium by a new, raised garden court. The foyer within the restored former Nebiolo building courtyard, itself encased in a new glazed structure, forms a voluminous internal space in which dynamic theatrical or concert performances could be staged.

At the heart of the scheme's organisation is its ability to engage with the public domain, encouraging the visitor to experience all aspects of the new complex, whether as inquisitive child, scholar or interested visitor, and to engage with those who merely wish to view the city from the entirely new dimension of the building's rooftop piazza.

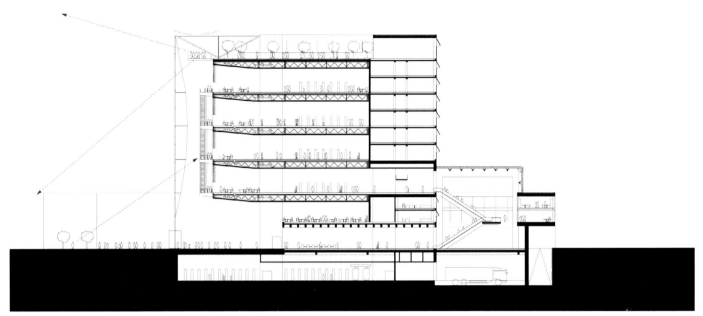

Section

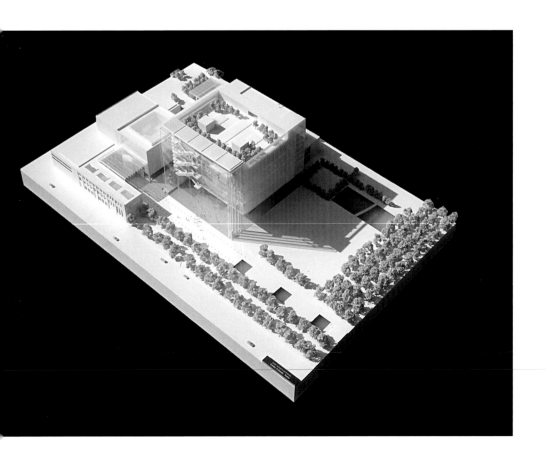

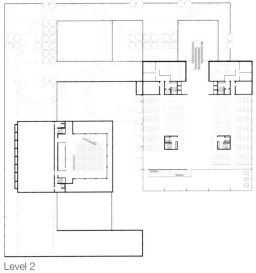

Level 2

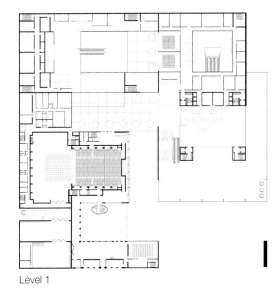

Level 1

Ground

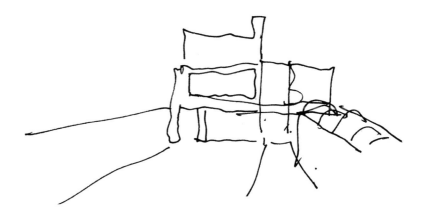

The Long House
London NW8, England, 2001–2005

The Long House, a radical new-build 720-square-metre home, was created for a private client in St John's Wood, an affluent suburb in north London. The house replaces two former dwellings that were separated by an 8-metre-wide vacant strip of land. Collectively forming the site, these three elements create a triangular land parcel bordered on the west side by an historic mews. Although there had been some post-war development and repair of bomb-damaged buildings, the site is set in a mature conservation area, thus a new-build, contemporary house is a very rare event.

The mews was originally built to service the grand villas on Hamilton Terrace immediately to the west. The triangular land parcel on which the new house sits forms the eastern side of the mews, sitting in marked contrast to the rectangular street and plot division typical of the neighbourhood. This triangularity is the result of a fault line of land ownership between two large London estates, the Eyre Estate and the Harrow, which form the historic land and building ownership. The western side of the mews is formed by double-storey, 19th-century terraced service buildings, now converted as upmarket dwellings that give the street the appearance of a single-sided London mews.

In contrast to the typology of the vicinity's typical large four- or five-storey houses, in which rooms are stacked vertically above one another, the Long House is low-build and has the luxury of large interconnected horizontal spaces on the main ground level. The composition of the 49-metre-long building has been determined by careful integration of the new masses with the scale and form of the existing adjoining urban condition. The house drops in scale from three storeys adjacent the terraced houses on Hill Road to the east to a single storey for both the garden wing and the connecting element between the main house, the guest wing and garage block.

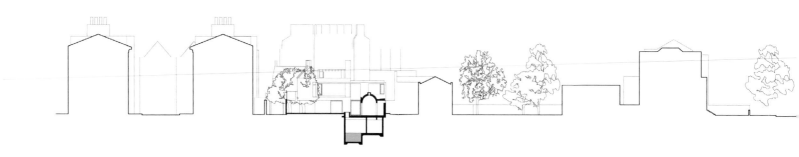

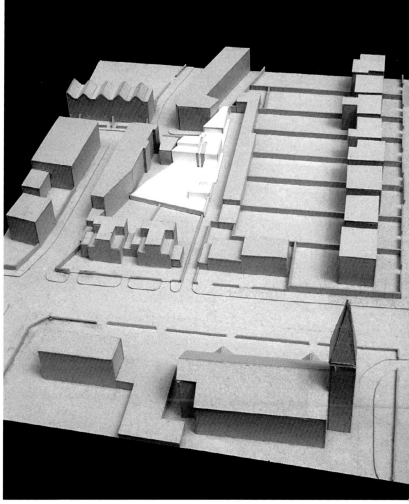

The Long House was conceived as a secret dwelling, so when viewed from the street it appears introverted and screened from the outside world. Internally, it comprises living and dining spaces, a top-lit subterranean lap pool and steam room, four main bedrooms, a guest and maid's wing and a garage for two cars.

Externally its flank to the mews is formed by the rebuilt, pre-existing garden boundary wall of English bond stock brickwork, surmounted by a clerestory glazed strip and zinc vault forming the garden wing. The smaller, upper portions of the house are formed of simple blank façades – one in white render and one in stock brick – that have been deployed along the top of the wall and echo the volumes of the earlier buildings. On the garden side, the elevations open out towards the garden's spaces in a freer and more transparent way, dissolving the relational contrasts between interior and exterior.

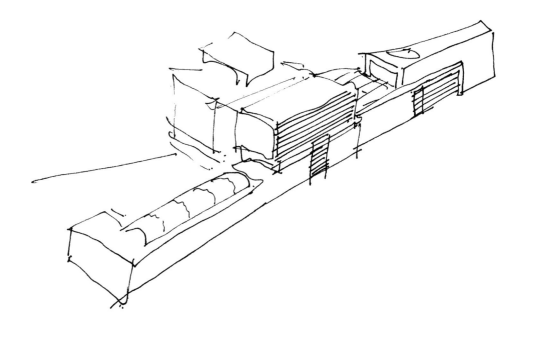

The external materials comprise stock brickwork, render and zinc, while the third-storey aedicule is in green pre-patinated copper. Interior materials include floors in oiled oak and Pietro Lauro limestone, the latter material extending outwards to form the exterior garden terrace surfaces.

Unsurprisingly, the project has had a protracted planning history with consent initially recommended by Westminster City Council's far-sighted planning officers, only for the scheme to fail at planning sub-committee stage at the hands of vigorous local opposition. A subsequent appeal to the Secretary of State's Inspectorate was upheld enabling the project to be realised.

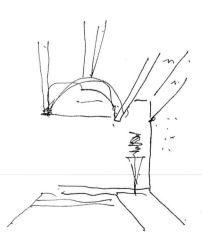

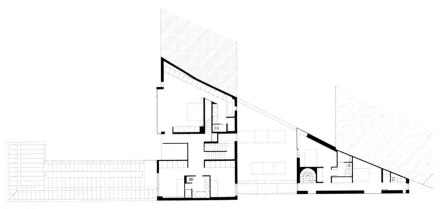

Level 1

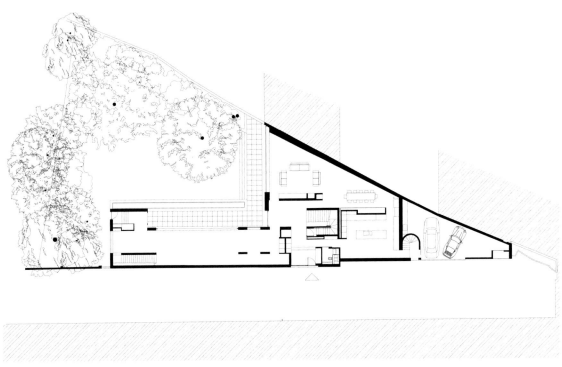

Ground

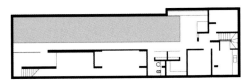

Lower ground

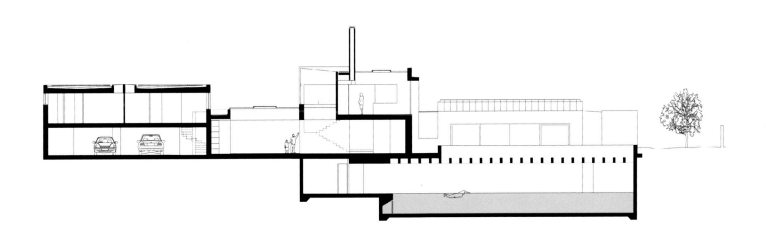

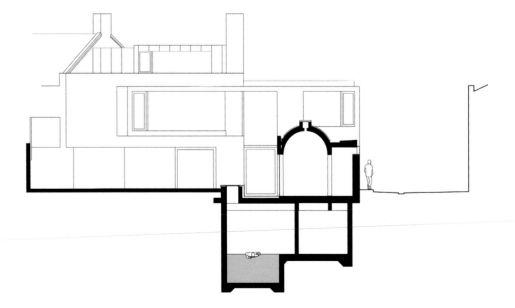

1   Fixed double-glazed roof light system
2   Exposed fair-faced concrete finish
3   Pre-patinated zinc standing seam cladding to roof and gutter
4   Foam glass insulation substrate with PC serrated clip fixings over bituminous primer
5   Zinc-lined gutter
6   Recessed luminaire
7   Folded zinc coping over STO rendered parapet
8   100 STO insulated render cladding
9   10-mm calcium silicate board substrate to STO insulated render along gutter detail
10   Render insulation to soffit and reveal
11   Powder-coated double-glazed aluminium sliding unit
12   40-mm-thick 600 x 600 Bateig blue limestone paving slabs
13   Adjustable Harmer plastic supports with 10-mm nom joints
14   20-mm limestone cladding supported on metal structure by stone S/c with mastic joints colour to match stone
15   75 extruded polystyrene insulation adhered to the RC upstand
16   RIW LAC waterproofing to upstand to overlap with mastic asphalt upstand
17   Clear laminated glass floor unit double glazed with 16-mm air gap
18   30-mm limestone coping on adhesive bed with downstand return
19   100-mm rainwater drain
20   6-mm marine ply fixed to face of sheet piles for backfilling with lean mix concrete
21   50-mm rigid polystyrene insulation board
22   RC basement structure watertight concrete
23   Two coats of waterproof render applied by specialist pool contractor
24   Glass mosaic finish
25   Recessed guide for electrically operated pool cover
26   Flat bottomed pool 20-mm glass mosaic tiled finish over waterproof render
27   Access panel to pool cover with mosaic finish
28   20-mm honed and sealed limestone on thin adhesive bed stone to pool surround
29   80-mm sand cement screed
30   Water-based underfloor heating-rigid insulation with preformed pockets for pipe location
31   Grille for air handling
32   20-mm oiled solid timber strip flooring bonded to sand cement screed with Winzer Würth wood flooring adhesive

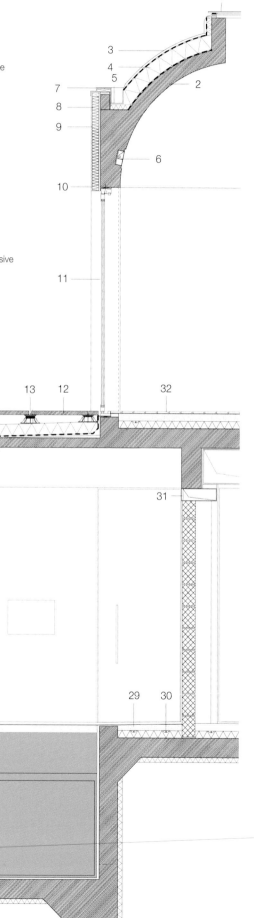

Athlone Civic Centre
Athlone, Ireland, 2001–2004

Athlone's new civic centre houses the town library, the Council's civic chamber, its administrative offices and a one-stop shop enabling the Council to effectively offer a single accessible point of contact with the public for all of its services.

The site for the new civic centre and square is in the eastern (Leinster/Westmeath) quarter of the town. Space for the project was created by demolishing the former council offices – an undistinguished house crudely extended in the 1970s and surrounded by rundown industrial premises. The strategic direction of the project was guided by Ireland's National Buildings Agency, which had drawn up a masterplan for the site. The project is located immediately north of the gothic St Mary's Church with its adjacent Jacobean Tower. It faces across the new town square and St Mary's cemetery towards Church Street, Athlone's historic main artery that leads down to the River Shannon and the traditional town centre.

The building is organised formally using four prime compositional elements. The huge, top-lit public entrance hall, from which access to all elements of the building can be gained, is immediately legible from the public square. It contains the ceremonial stair to the debating chamber and is the key organising space within the building. Immediately to its right, when viewed from the new square, is the one-stop shop with a debating chamber located above. To the left are two bar-like forms – the lower of the two contains the double-height library and the upper contains the administrative offices on two levels. For the most part, the project is naturally ventilated to provide the necessary cooling to most of the office and library spaces, while reconstructed stone louvres on the south elevation both reinforce the architectural language and provide solar shading during summer, thereby allowing the building to have a relatively low energy requirement.

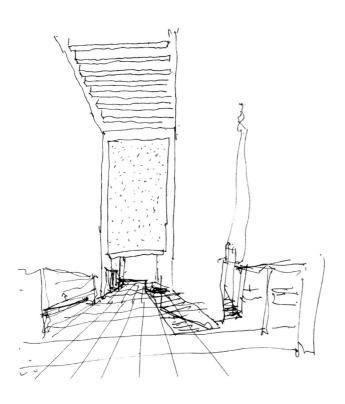

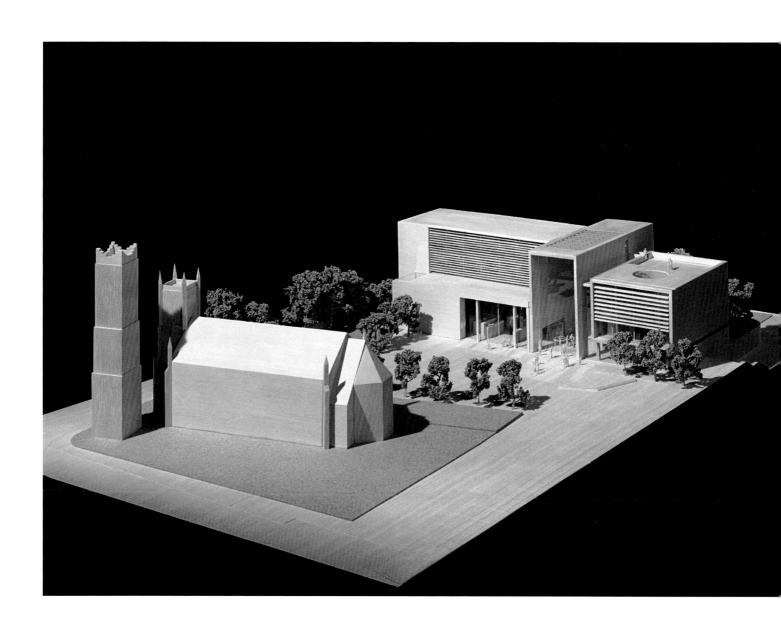

The civic centre is built from a form of pale, honed, reconstructed stone, a material that echoes Athlone's major stone-built public structures: the Castle, the grand neo-baroque Church of St Peter and St Paul (1937) and Shannon Bridge. Each major public structure, despite being built at different times in different architectural styles for very different purposes, exhibits a solid, formal consistency that distinguishes the civic buildings from the traditional architecture of the town, which is largely rough stucco roofed in natural pitched slate. The designs for the civic centre follow that developmental pattern. Remnants of the former town wall and bastion dating from the 17th century were identified during site investigation and were restored and integrated into the construction of the new town square.

The project involved the Williams office at every design level, from the elaboration of the urban proposition through to the minutiae of the interior. The firm designed the bespoke joinery for the Council chamber, created a new design for the public benches for the civic square and designed and patented a range of interior door furniture, the Parallel Range, specifically for the project.

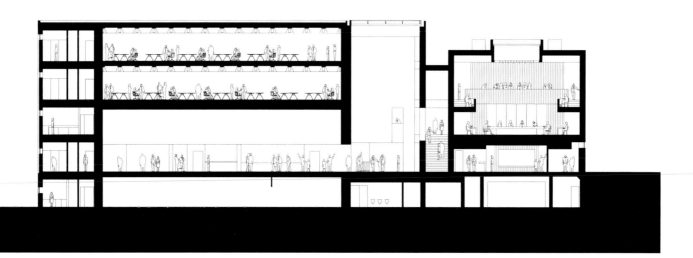

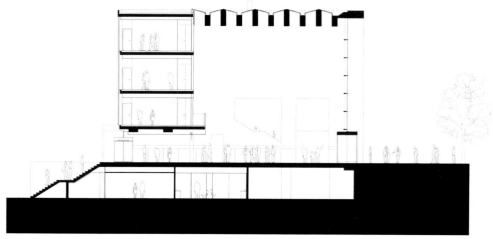

Section through atrium

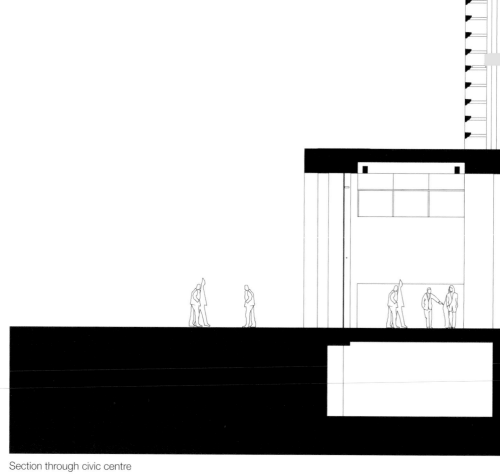

Section through civic centre

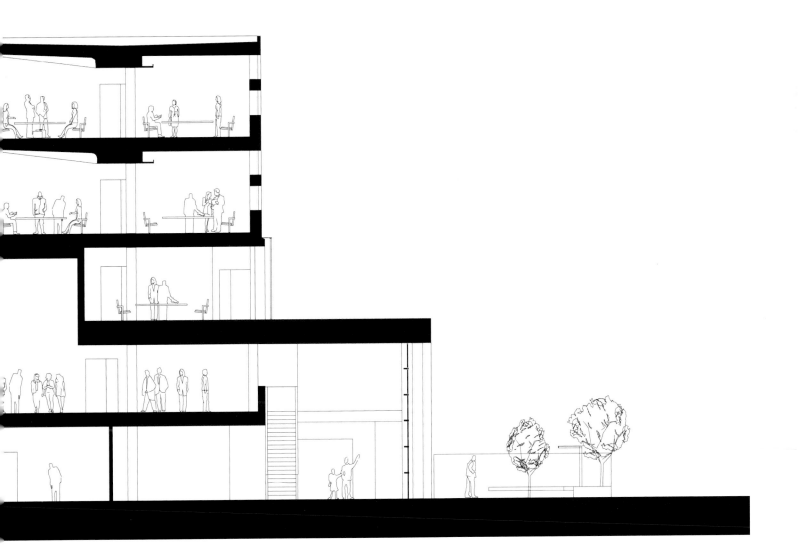

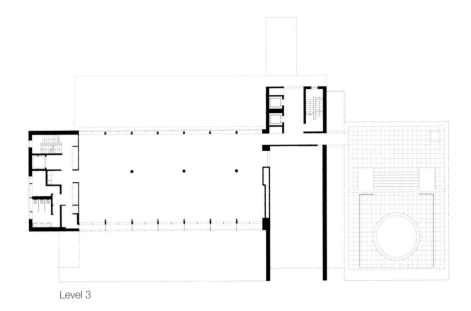

Level 3

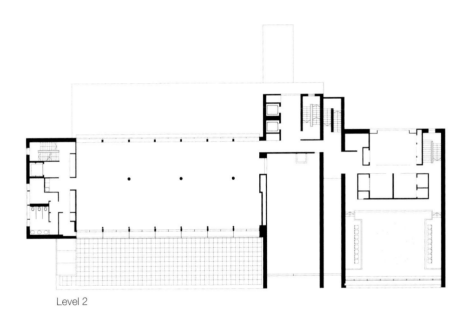

Level 2

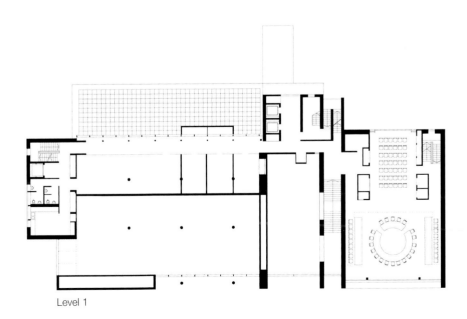

Level 1

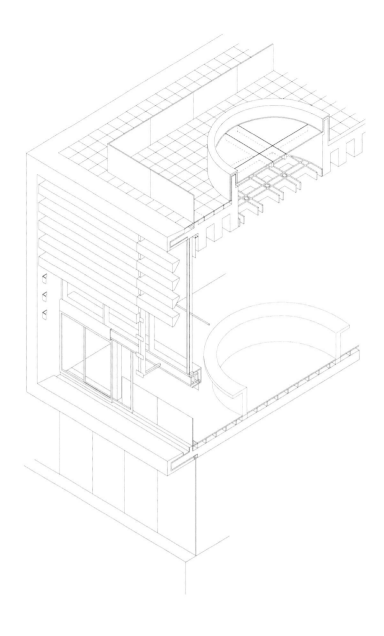

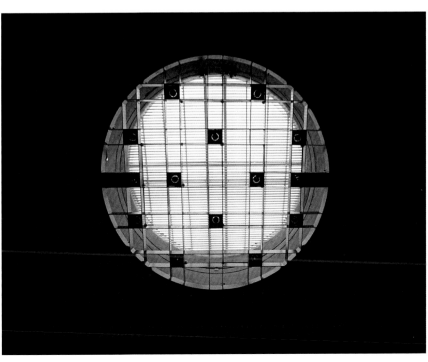

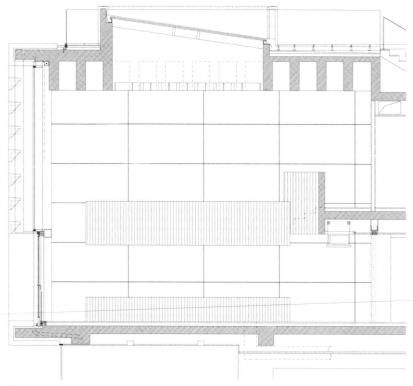

Chamber section

The Unicorn Theatre
London SE1, England, 2001–2005

The Unicorn Theatre for children and young people is located on Tooley Street, near London Bridge and the River Thames. The Unicorn is the only new central London theatre to be built since the National in 1976. It houses a 320-seat theatre, a studio theatre, education, teaching and rehearsal spaces, a public foyer and café and is the most far-reaching, child-focused educative and theatrical institution in the UK.

Founded in 1947 by Caryl Jenner, the Unicorn began life touring in two ex-MOD trucks. From 1967 it shared space at the Arts Theatre in Covent Garden before vacating in 1999 to acquire a permanent base of its own. In late 2000 the Unicorn launched a Europe-wide architectural competition, which was won by Keith Williams.

Williams' winning designs were influenced by artistic director Tony Graham's groundbreaking theatrical work, but also derive from a rigorous assimilation of the internal program, a careful attitude towards the new building's context and the opportunity to treat the project's formal composition sculpturally.

The resultant building grew from a five-year collaboration between Williams' office and the Unicorn Theatre. It must be 'rough yet beautiful', to recall Graham's opening remarks when first briefing his architect. In urban terms, the new Unicorn continues the varied scale of existing buildings along Tooley Street, with Foster + Partners' much larger, glazed office buildings as its backdrop, separating it from the Thames.

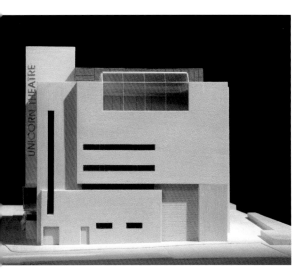

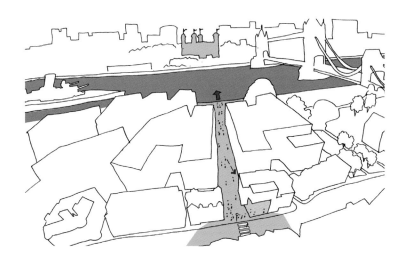

Unicorn.
Theatre

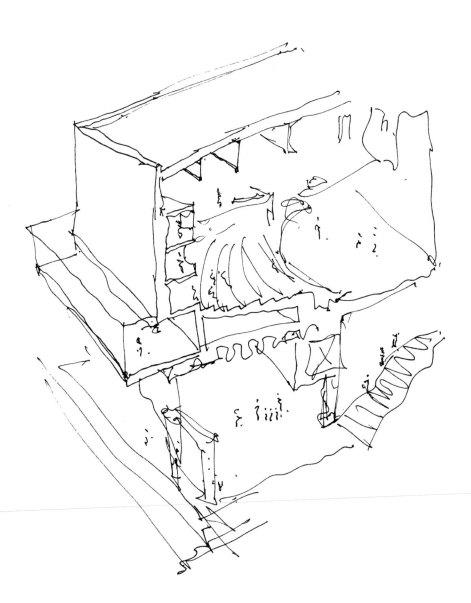

That the architecture is deliberately equivocal adds to its richness. The new building is an asymmetric pavilion. Its elevations are open and transparent where they need to be, revealing the heart of the building to the public, yet elsewhere are deliberately solid and cliff-like, punctuated by carefully controlled window openings and top lighting. This approach recognises a dynamic future as well as the architectural precedent of this part of London – the narrow streets and warehouses that once occupied the site and the nearby 19th-century railway viaducts of London Bridge station.

The L-shaped foyer presents a glazed transparent front along both Tooley Street and the serendipitously named Unicorn Passage, the pedestrianised route to the River Thames. The foyer is multilevel and transparent, revealing both the studio theatre and the grand stair, which leads to the Weston Theatre (the main auditorium) 7 metres above. Clad in pre-oxidised copper panels, the main auditorium balances spectacularly above the foyer and Unicorn Passage.

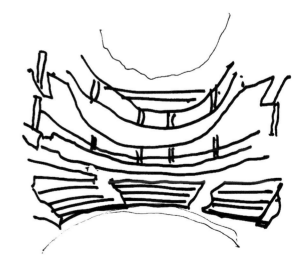

The materials are freely but precisely arranged, reinforcing the building masses that coalesce to form abstract asymmetrical sculptural compositions for each elevation. The copper cladding of the Weston Theatre contrasts with the blue-glazed brick faience that surrounds the stage door. Bright stucco and blue engineering brick are used elsewhere.

The larger architectural gestures of the spectacularly projecting main auditorium and the mannerist corner tower with its eroded base signal the new building at an urban level, yet the designs are rich in child-scale detail. The stages, balconies, seating and in particular the form of the main auditorium itself are derived from narrative story telling, and all bring a delicate and appropriate scale to a unique new theatre for children.

The 3650-square-metre theatre was opened by Lord Attenborough to huge critical acclaim on 1 December 2005, and among many awards the building was shortlisted for the penultimate round of the 2006 Stirling Prize.

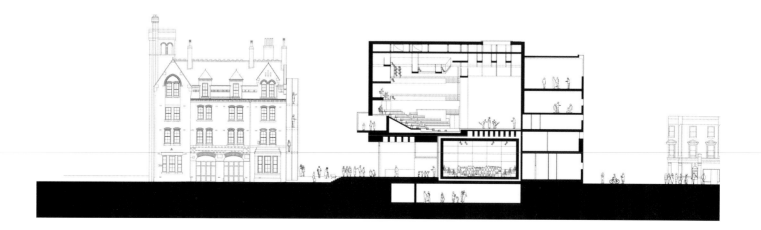

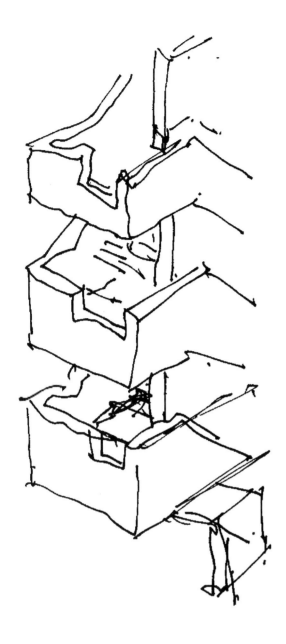

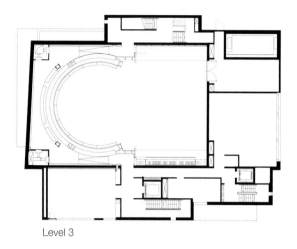

Level 3

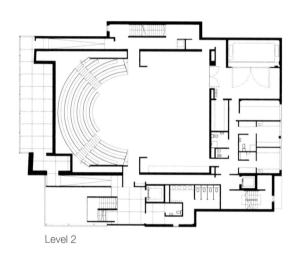

Level 2

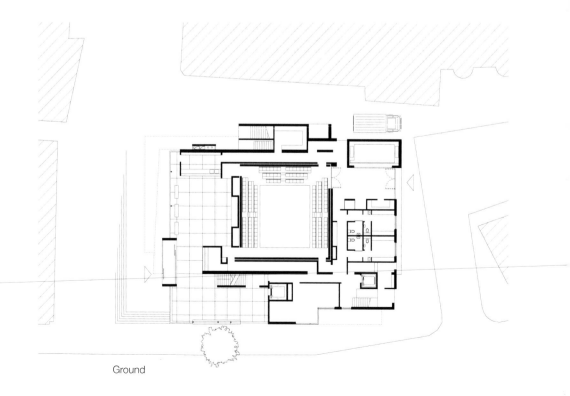

Ground

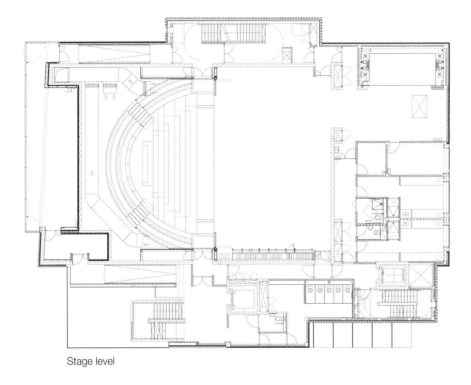

Stage level

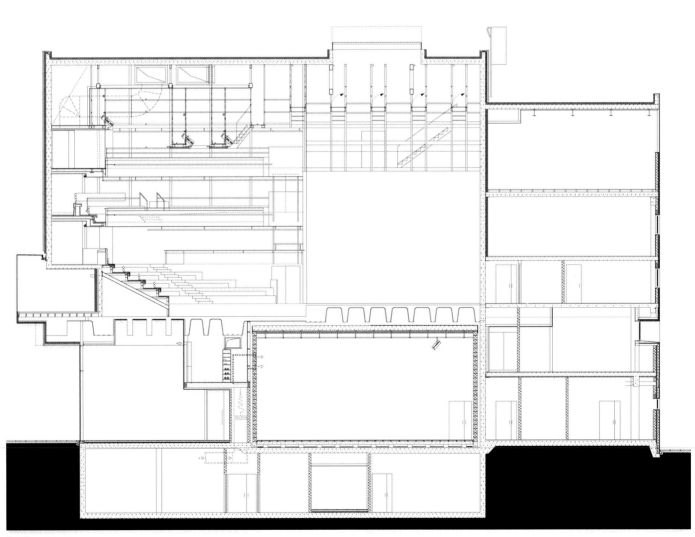

Section

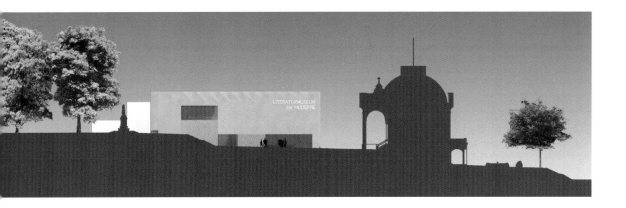

Literaturmuseum der Moderne
Marbach am Neckar, Germany, 2001

Marbach am Neckar was the birthplace in 1751 of Friedrich von Schiller, the great poet, philosopher and dramatist. The Schiller Museum, a neo-baroque building opened in 1903, sits on a spectacular site atop an escarpment overlooking the River Neckar. The invited project for the new Museum of Literature included a series of public galleries, and seminar and research spaces sitting alongside the existing museum within a new wing, separate above ground but linked at subterranean level. The scheme comprised a major public foyer and a sequence of differing gallery spaces for both temporary and permanent collections.

A study centre and archive dating from 1972, composed in a fractured organic plan form, was built offset to one side of the central axis of the baroque museum. In Williams' project, the new 1400-square-metre Schiller wing forms a complementary though compositionally different, isolated pavilion that creates a new architectural ensemble with the existing museum and its forecourt. The design is an attempt to re-balance and complete the tripartite composition with the main museum and study centre around a general symmetrical organising axis that emanates from the 1903 building.

Conceptually, the project is seen as a foil to the existing building. Its textural nature is very different in that its surfaces are clad in a seamless fritted glazed system that sits on a podium base. Controlled top lighting illuminates key points within the plan, including the gallery and grand stair, while diffused sidelight gives an abstract, contemplative character to the main entry and foyer gallery. A processional stair in a triple-height volume drives through the various gallery levels of the plan, anchoring the public vertical circulation as a key reference point within the interior spatial sequence.

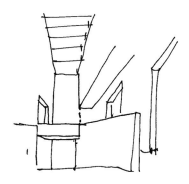

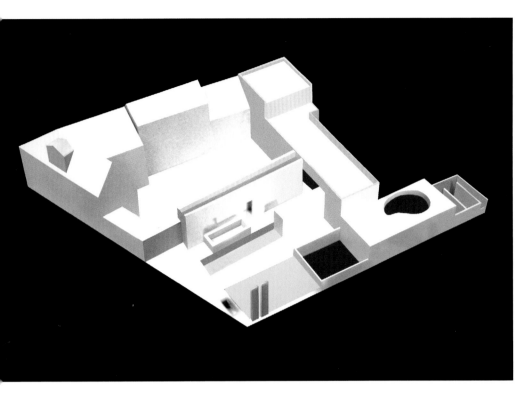

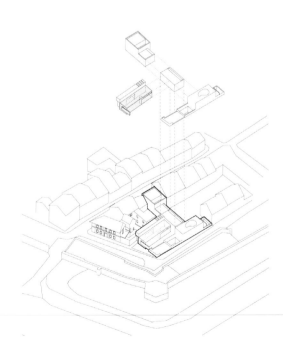

Nietzsche Archive
Naumburg, Germany, 2002

The invited project for the adaptation and extension to Nietzsche's former house in Naumburg set out to establish a new documentation and study centre for recording, displaying and analysing the life and work of the great philosopher. The documentation centre contains gallery and study spaces as well as support facilities for the public. The project was conceived not as a building but as a series of architectonic events taking place within the recognisable typology of a suburban villa and garden, in this case Nietzsche's relatively modest house.

Such a framework allowed the primacy of the main house as the site of Nietzsche's intellectual and domestic activity to be maintained, while the new intervention set out to be a 'non-building' by sidestepping the issue of appropriateness of a new façade, choosing instead to relate the new structures to more primal forces of light, landscape and water.

The new centre is reached through a linear reception hall, which contains the main entrance, the connection to the rear courtyard of the existing Nietzsche house and the more casual public spaces such as the café, shop and ticketing. The café has two characters – one set deeper into the plan is more formal and overlooks the double-height exhibition space below, the other is more relaxed and relates directly to the external spaces to the east and features sliding glazed panels opening out in fine weather.

Despite its spatial richness, the scheme is in essence extremely simple. The main accommodation is organised in an L-shaped plan form rotated at 4 degrees to the reception hall, which acts rather like an armature by providing the underlying formal organisation in plan, while locking the scheme into the geometry of the site.

The main exhibition, study and research spaces are subterranean and are accessed by stair or lift. The exhibition and reading spaces are contained within top-lit halls. These are spaces of stark simplicity that make a connection to a perceived higher order in a distinctly secular yet quasi-numinous sequence of spaces. The interconnecting spaces are fluid, encouraging a less formal interaction between the different uses within the building and stimulating dialogue and consideration of Nietzsche's life and work in more contemplative manner.

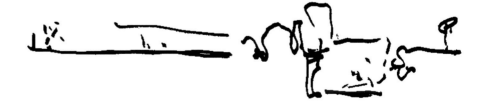

Parc & Dare Theatre and Arts Centre
Treorchy, Wales, 2004–2005

The Grade II* listed Parc & Dare Theatre, located in the former Rhondda Valley mining town of Treorchy, is formed from two buildings of very different architectural styles. Together, the former Workmen's Institute (1892) and the rock-faced, ashlar, neo-classical, 700-seat Parc & Dare Theatre (1913) form the town's major landmark.

The construction of the buildings was funded by subscriptions from the local miners, and consequently the Parc & Dare Theatre named after the two local collieries, has a very strong social and historic connection with the local community. The two buildings are listed Grade II* and, aside from the main auditorium, have been much altered internally.

Treorchy's town plan follows a linear low-rise form, with the main street running parallel to the River Rhondda, punctuated by occasional east–west crossing points. This project proposed the refurbishment of the existing buildings and the addition of a new arts wing to create a multivalent arts centre. The extension contains a new visual arts gallery, a 150-seat second auditorium space, a rehearsal room and dance studio, bars, and café and foyer spaces. The new build element occupies a dramatic location perched on the riverbank alongside the road bridge, creating a new landmark in the townscape.

The two existing buildings, although separated by only 20 years in design and construction, are fundamentally different in terms of scale and architectural language. This new arts wing consists of a simple stack of spaces forming the third architectural component of the tripartite building composition. The two existing Parc & Dare buildings were separated by a service yard and alleyway between them, which was used in the project to create a light-glazed slot containing a multi-storey circulation spine connecting the existing theatre to the new arts wing. The side walls of the slot were to be restored only where essential, leaving behind the scars of the removed structures and thereby revealing the past history of the building.

Williams' overall design strategy sought to preserve and re-invigorate the Parc & Dare for future generations and to add a vibrant new set of opportunities for artistic endeavours for the town, the region and beyond.

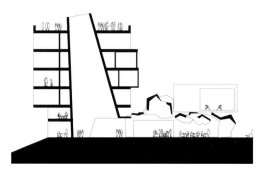

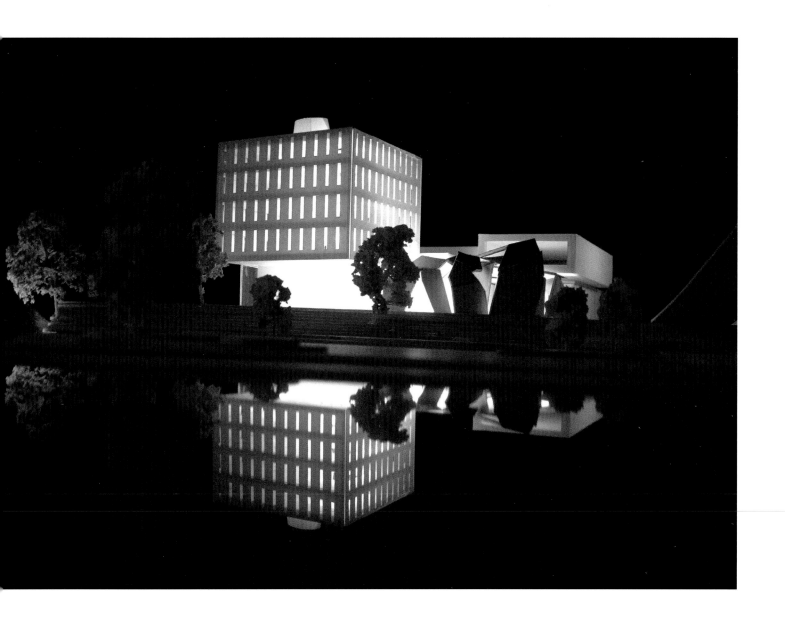

Irish World Music Centre (IWMC)
Limerick, Ireland, 2004

The project for the new 4350-square-metre teaching centre for music and dance (IWMC) for the University of Limerick explored the potential for a symbolic connection between music, dance, architecture and landscape for a new campus building on the edge of the River Shannon.

The project's architectural composition responds to both the rigid structure inherent in Western classical music and the spontaneous fluidity that characterises the development of much Irish folk-based music and dance. The project's massing is organised into three primary components – the armature containing all of the social and movement spaces, the performance space wing and the teaching cube – with the latter forming a key vertical marker at the arrival point of a new footbridge across the Shannon from the southern university campus.

The armature aside, the interior of the IWMC is seen in part as introspective, contemplative and studious, hence the predominance of top lighting, side lighting and clerestory lighting. The armature flows through both the plan and section connecting all key elements of the complex and at the same time provides sheltered internal pedestrian routing through the campus in inclement weather.

Reprising in miniature a similar move in the 2001 Centro Culturale di Torino design, a roof terrace atop the teaching cube offers a small-scale performance space and fine views across the Shannon toward the southern campus.

The teaching cube is clad in raw treated timber rainscreen planking on the main elevations, while hardwood 'eyelids' and vertical brise soleils provide solar screening to the south and west façades. The armature is enclosed with zinc-clad cranked plates forming the fractals with interstices between the panels and closed with solar shaded glazing. The performance space wing is clad in storey-height panels of polished concrete.

The broad landscape strategy bridges the extremes of a hard, semi-urban edge to the east at the arrival point of the new footbridge, breaking down to the natural beauty of the Shannon banks, enveloping a formal set piece of an outdoor grass banked amphitheatre facing south towards the river for summer outdoor performances.

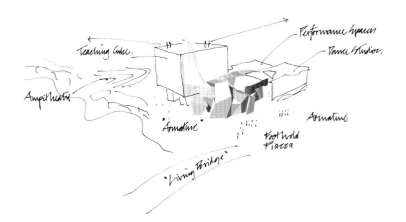

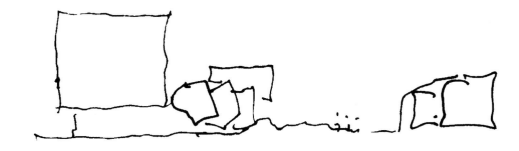

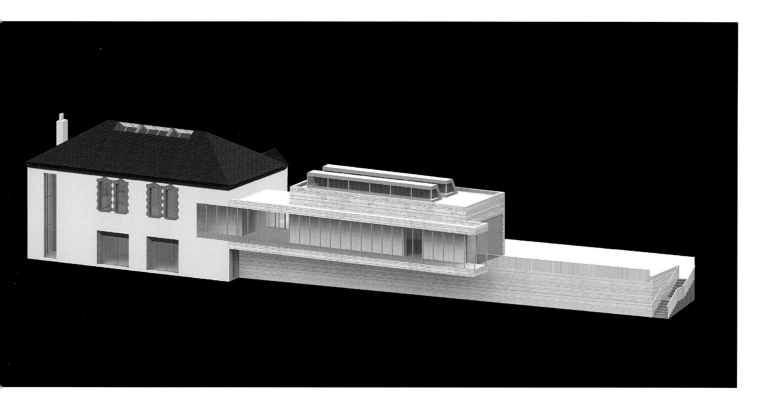

Athlone Art Gallery
Athlone, Ireland, 2006–2010

The project for Athlone's new 630-square-metre gallery for contemporary art is located on a spectacular site by the town's historic bridge, castle and the Catholic church of St Peter & St Paul. The scheme involves the adaptation of the historic 1897 Father Matthew Hall into a gallery, with a new wing added to provide temporary white box gallery spaces and a river gallery overlooking the Shannon.

Built to designs by William Tanner in 1897, the original Father Matthew Hall was commissioned as a temperance hall. It was hoped through providing a centre offering recreational facilities and a temperance café that workers from the nearby woollen mills would eschew the public house and remain sober.

Subsequently, the hall became a concert venue and then in 1947 it was handed over to Athlone Town Council. The upper floor of the building was used as the town hall until 1949, when a branch library opened on the ground floor. In 1980 the entire building was renovated and re-opened as a library, but has been vacant since 2004 following the library's relocation to Keith Williams' new Civic Centre.

The proposals retain but radically alter the Father Matthew Hall, while the new wing will provide contemporary gallery space with blackout capabilities to enable a multiuse gallery, lecture theatre, cinema for film exhibitions, meeting space for literature, music and drama workshops, and digital art exhibitions. The Father Matthew Hall will be stripped back internally to its brickwork to create a rugged shell in which to display art in a visually powerful and raw interior. The two buildings will be linked by a glazed entrance from the main road and by a linear river gallery facing the Shannon.

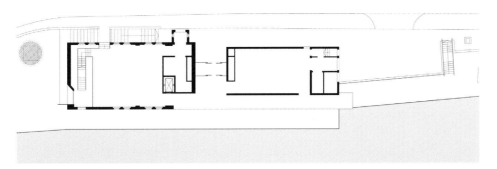

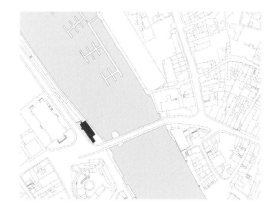

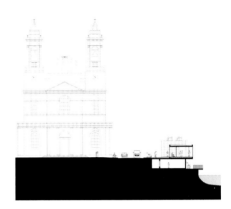

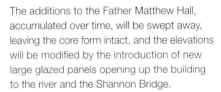

The additions to the Father Matthew Hall, accumulated over time, will be swept away, leaving the core form intact, and the elevations will be modified by the introduction of new large glazed panels opening up the building to the river and the Shannon Bridge.

The palette of materials for the new gallery wing is limited to limestone and zinc. Limestone as a building material has a history of use in public buildings in Ireland, and here the material will be laid in rough-cut horizontal strips of varying widths asserting the contemporary nature of the new wing. Zinc-clad roof lanterns will be set back from the parapet wall to allow the limestone to have prominence in the façade while also centralising the light penetrating into the gallery. The Father Matthew Hall will be re-rendered and the existing roof replaced with a new roof structure and natural slate tiles. The project, when opened in 2010, will be the firm's second major project for Athlone Town Council, after the Athlone Civic Centre, 2001–2004.

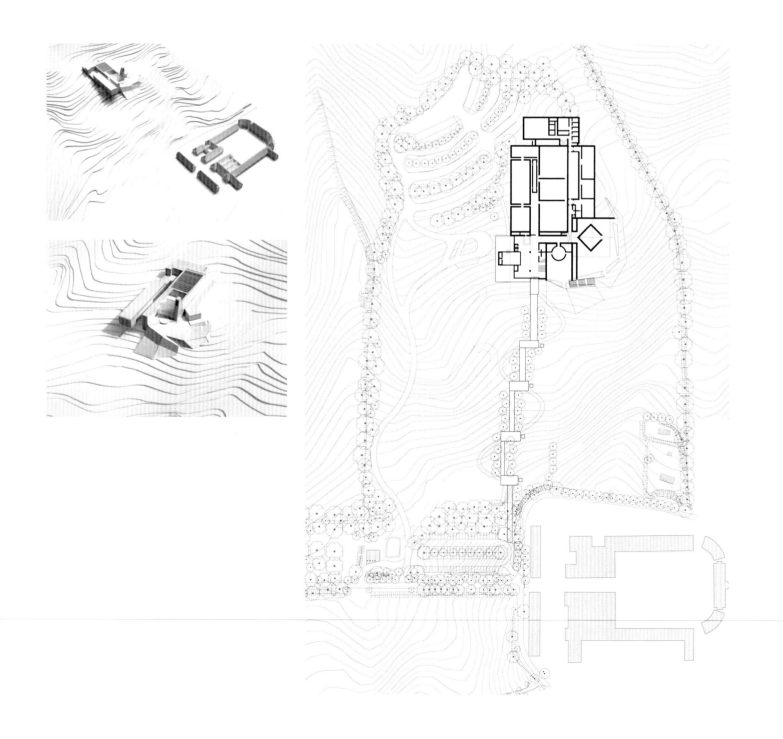

Moesgård Museum of Cultural History
Århus, Denmark, 2005

Keith Williams Architects was the only UK firm invited to prepare designs in a limited international competition for the new 15,500-square-metre Moesgård Museum of Cultural History near Århus in Denmark. The competition was jointly promoted by the Museum and the University of Århus.

Located within the Moesgård Estate, once an 18th-century manor house and the now the existing Moesgård Ethnography Museum with extensive land bordering the sea at Århus Bugt (the Bay of Århus), Williams sited the proposed Museum on a natural plateau towards the northern end of the site, ensuring that the building would enjoy the best views across both the former manor house and its landscape. Williams also felt that the sculptural composition of the proposed building should be evident in the skyline and exploit the potential to place key spaces within the museum complex to offer distant views to the sea. As a consequence, the new building appears as an acropolis – a dynamic pavilion emerging from the sensuous, undulating landscape.

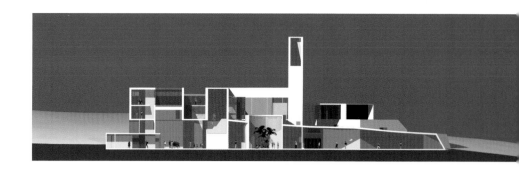

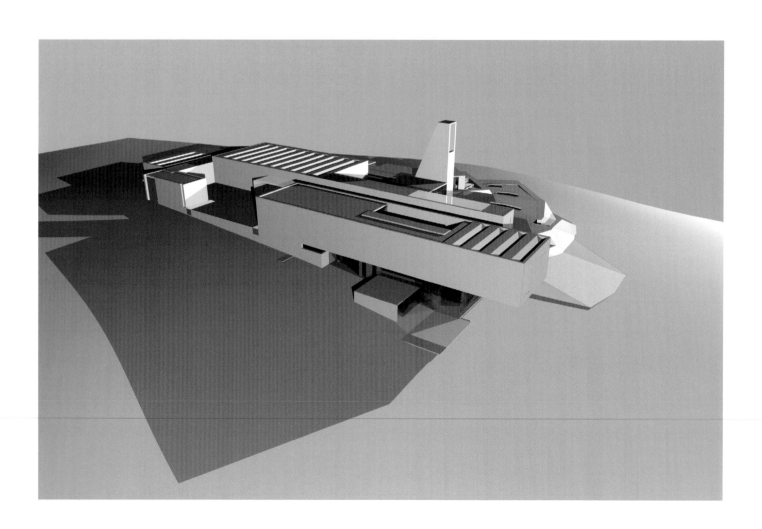

The Moesgård Museum project contains a variety of exemplary flexible galleries and exhibition spaces, principally Pre-Historic and Medieval Denmark Galleries, Arabian Gulf Galleries, Ethnographic Exhibition Spaces and temporary exhibition galleries in an interior that contains a rich series of noble and beautiful spaces.

The estate grounds contain buildings and structures of historic human activity. The Museum was therefore seen as a rich repository of history and artefacts in context with the wider landscape. The project is one part of a broader journey that connects the new Museum, the Historisk eksperimentarium, the 18th-century Manor House, the formal garden and the woods surrounding a restored water mill as a series of components within a single entity. The layout in plan of the Museum complex takes inspiration from the elegant simplicity of the former Moesgård manor and its outbuildings. The planning brought about an architecture of linear strips that, though axial about the original main house, is asymmetrically disposed on the site.

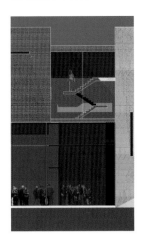

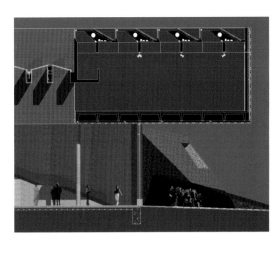

In terms of materiality, the western approach façades were largely made from red/brown brick echoing the colour and construction of the existing Moesgård Museum buildings, while the central section was proposed in honed aggregate pre-cast concrete panels. The cranked boundary wall was made from rough limestone blocks and the modular bar, integrated with the sculpted grass bank forming the eastern edge, was topped with glazed pavilions housing the main administration and education facilities.

The use of materials reinforced the gradation of architectural form, from the hard western edge through to the softening of the architectural form as it dissolved into the landscape at its eastern flank. The Museum's forms also expressed the contrast between the manmade and the natural, the hard western edge at visitor approach becomes gradually diffuse as it connects with the landscape and vista to the south and east, rooting the building in the hillside.

Level 1

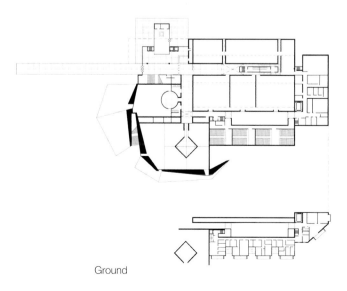

Ground

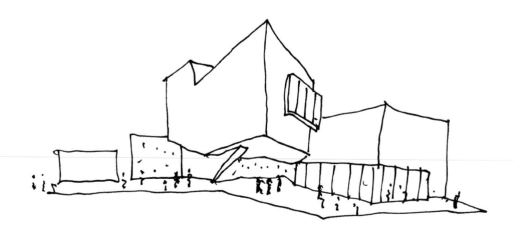

Kunstens Hus
Herning, Denmark, 2005

The project, which the organisers described as an artistic lighthouse for central Jutland, called for a new-build, 7000-square-metre museum and arts centre to provide temporary exhibition spaces and permanent galleries for housing important works by Piero Manzoni, sculptor Ingvar Cronhammar and constructivist Paul Gadegaard, among others. The brief also required the building to provide a base for the MidWest Ensemble, comprising a 150-seat recital hall, rehearsal spaces and public and administrative areas.

The project's organising concept envisaged a tension between the ordered neutrality of the displayed art spaces and the moving dynamic of music. Architecturally and programmatically, this idea resulted in a formal schism between the two art forms that was manifested in the rectilinear grid of the main gallery spaces and the more complex skewed geometry of the concert hall.

The overarching formal composition of the project was ordered by the geometry of the nearby Carl-Henning Pedersen & Else Alfelt Museum and the split formed by the angled entrance to Pedersen's Wheel of Life mural. These geometries connected the new Kunstens Hus symbolically to the existing galleries and ordered the composition of the new elements.

The shimmering metal-clad concert hall at first floor level appears to float in space, acting as both a sculptural symbol of the new Kunstens Hus and a portal to the new south-facing public square beyond. It sits in deliberate contrast to the massive ground-rooted nature of the brick and concrete architecture of the top-lit gallery spaces. The third element, the glazed foyer, connects the former two components.

The galleries, foyer and concert hall face south to a new public square and amphitheatre. The character of the temporary and permanent exhibition galleries is distinct and reflects the different nature of the art they will display, with the two forms gradually melding at their confluence.

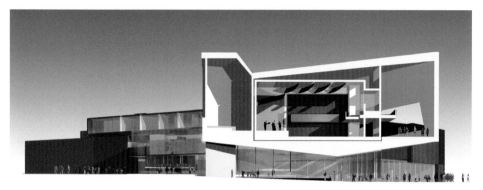

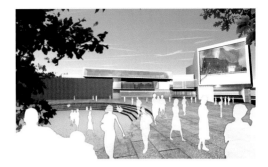

Level 2

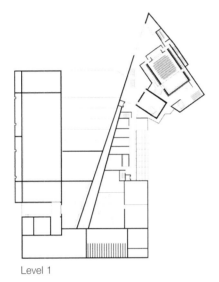

Level 1

Ground

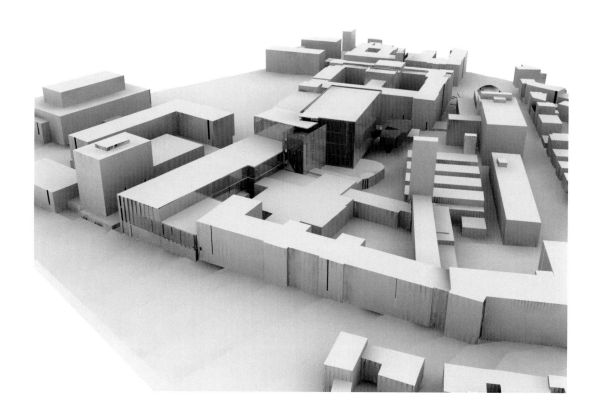

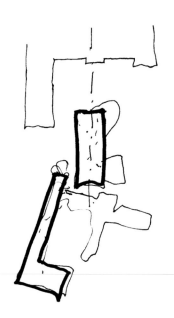

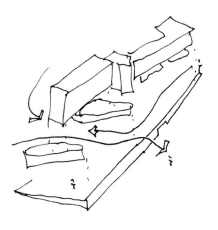

Universitäts und Landesbibliothek
TU Darmstadt, Germany, 2005

The project involved the insertion of a new 30,000-square-metre university library amid the central TU Darmstadt campus buildings. The library was conceived as a pair of shimmering crystalline bars, or wings, floating through the fractured campus buildings and spaces above a new landscaped dais that unites pedestrian ground-level movement through the campus.

Architecturally, the crystalline rigour of the new buildings distinguishes them from the existing campus structures, and the library is characterised as the central knowledge repository, literally and symbolically at the heart of the university.

The new library is formally organised in two wings. The first stitches into the fractured group of buildings and spaces adjacent the parking ramp, and the second takes the form of a promontory or pier. Aligned on the central section of the Hauptebäude, the main 19th-century campus, the new library floats over the free-form ground-level spaces that contain the entrance foyer and the staff areas, which separate it from the solid plate of the dais at ground level.

The two wings are jointed at an architectural armature at the connection point with the Schlossgarten. The armature contains the major vertical circulation for all public and student library levels. The double-level dais, over which the northern wing floats, provides a new uniting platform within the heart of the campus and connects the main ground levels of all university buildings to one another, with Alexanderstrasse at its southwest corner.

In the context of the campus, the new library is conceived as a jewel-like object set within the collar of existing buildings. Somewhat taller than surrounding buildings, the new library is imagined as a shimmering form within the campus heart when seen from afar.

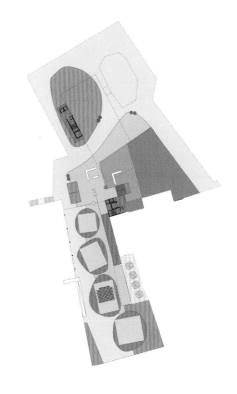

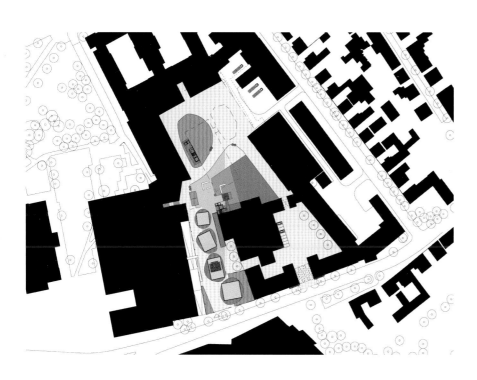

Wexford Opera House
Ireland, 2005–2008

Wexford Festival Opera is as important culturally to Ireland as the Glyndebourne Festival is to England. Consequently, the building of the new 7235-square-metre Wexford Opera House, a joint project between Keith Williams Architects and the Irish Government's Office of Public Works architects department, is Ireland's most important arts project of recent years.

The new opera house was constructed in the heart of the medieval maritime town, on the site of the Festival's former theatre. It comprises the new main 780-seat opera house, full flytower and backstage and a transformable, second, 175-seat space, together with rehearsal, production facilities, bars, café and foyer spaces.

Close up, the new building has retained the extraordinary elements of surprise and secrecy – so characteristic of the old Theatre Royal – by re-integrating itself, behind reinstated terraced buildings, into the historic fabric of Wexford's medieval centre. The scale of the building and its contribution to Wexford's silhouette only becomes truly apparent when the project is viewed from the banks of the River Slaney. From there the new flytower appears in the skyline alongside the spires of Wexford's two Pugin-inspired churches and the Italianate tower of the Franciscan Friary, announcing the presence of an exceptional new cultural building in the historic townscape.

Kzrysztof Szumanski as 'Frost' in the WFO 2008 production *Snegurochka* by Rimsky-Korsakov

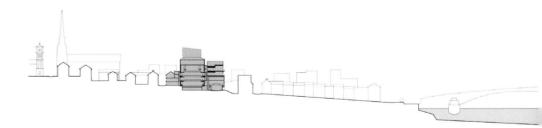

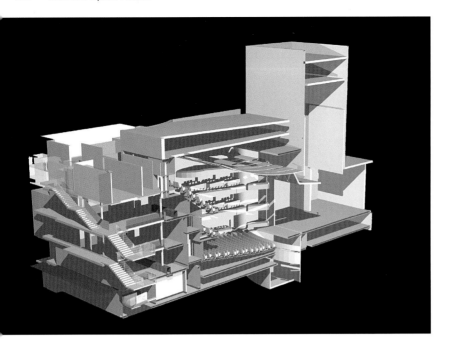

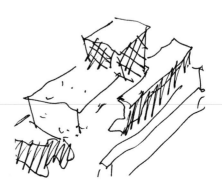

Internally, the main auditorium, inspired both by the form of a cello and the curves of a traditional horseshoe operatic space, has been lined in North American black walnut while the seating has been finished in pale purple leather, lending it a rich sense of material quality. Though primarily conceived for the autumn opera festival, the new building is intended to operate as a year-round arts venue for additional Wexford Festival productions and visiting companies.

Officially opened by Mr Brian Cowen TD An Taoiseach, the Irish Prime Minister, on 5 September 2008, the first opera in this award-winning new house was staged on 16 October 2008 with a performance of Rimsky-Korsakoff's *Snegourchka* (the *Snow Maiden*).

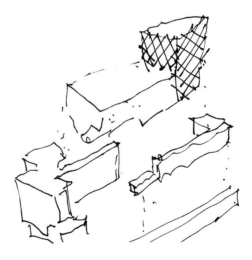

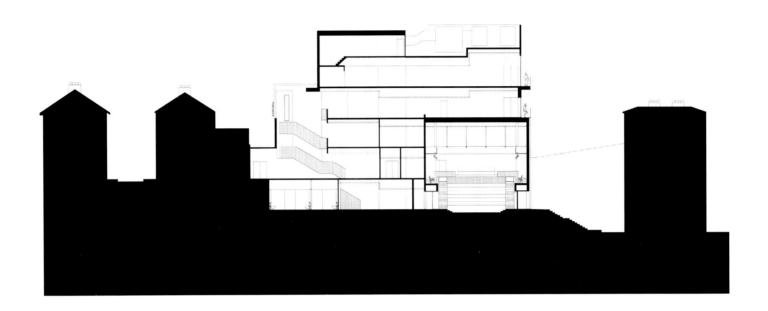

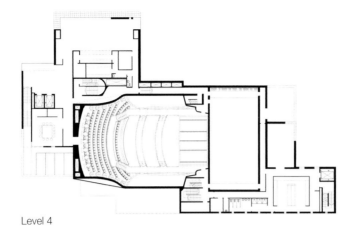

Level 4

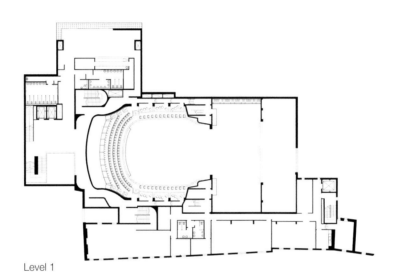

Level 1

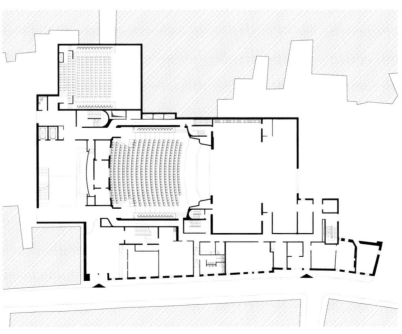

Ground

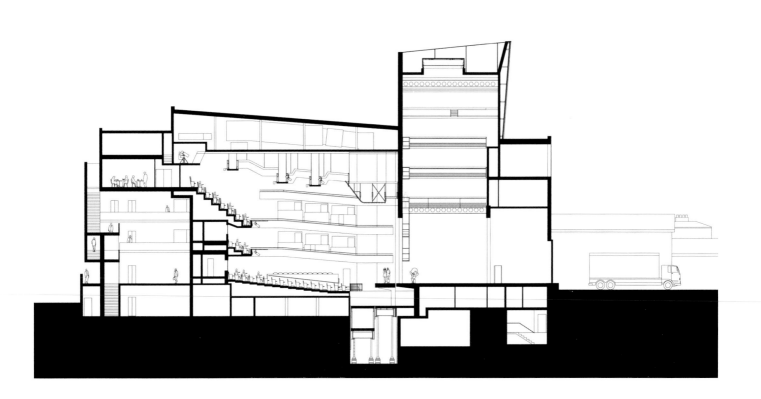

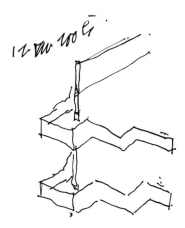

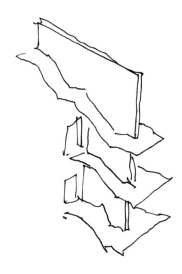

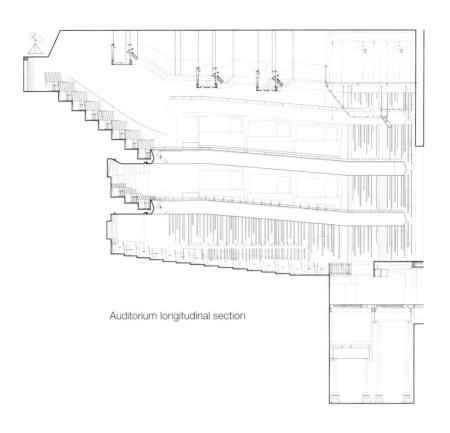

Auditorium longitudinal section

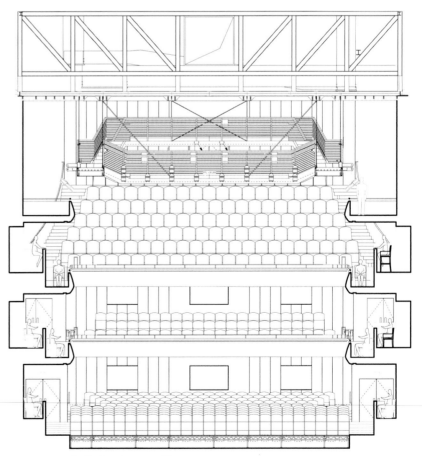

Auditorium cross section

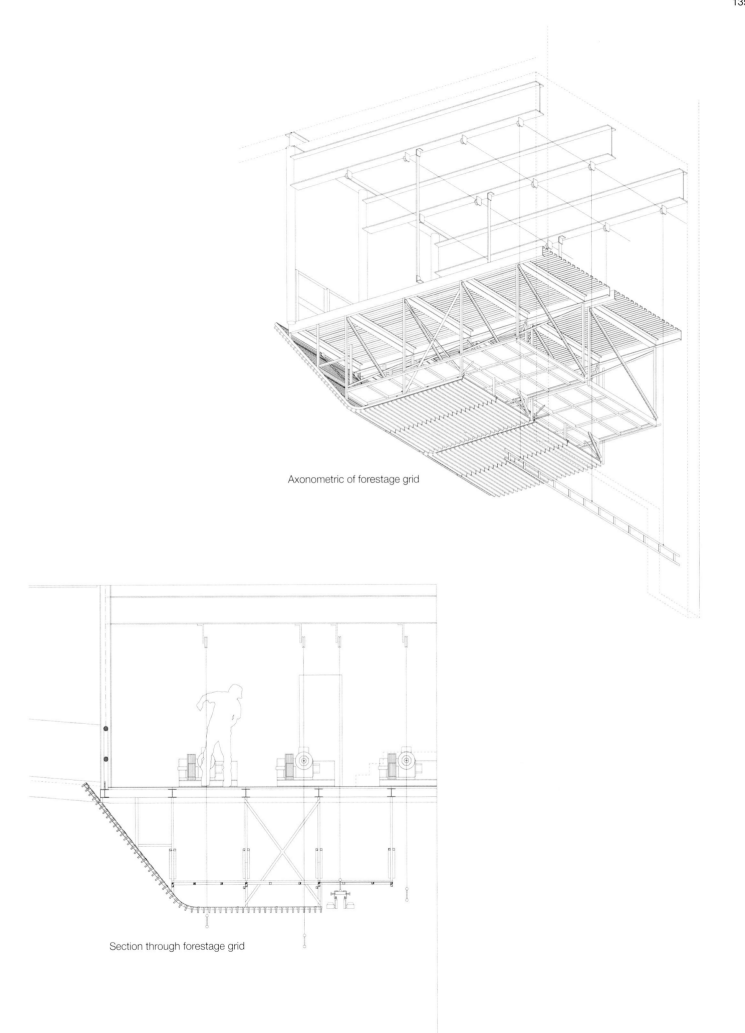

Axonometric of forestage grid

Section through forestage grid

Irina Samoylova and Natela Nicoli in the 2008 WFO production
Snegurochka by Rimsky-Korsakov

The Jerome Hynes Theatre – 176 seats

The Jerome Hynes Theatre – seats retracted

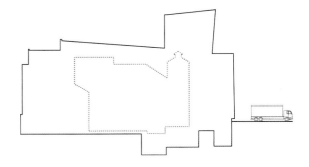

The diagrammatic section shows the scale relationship between the old Theatre Royal and the new Opera House. The photographs show the old and new auditoriums at approximately the same scale.

Contrast of scale between old and new auditorium

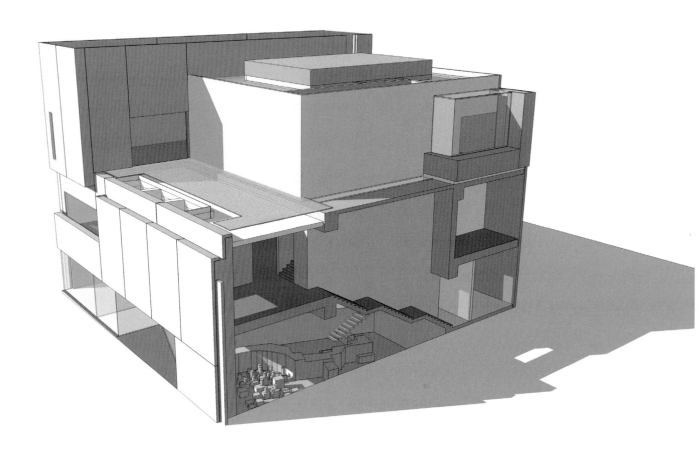

Chichester District Museum
Chichester, England, 2007–2011

The city plan of Chichester is characterised by a ring of largely intact enveloping medieval walls, within which the older city is segmented into four roughly equal quadrants by a cruciform street pattern centred upon a medieval market cross. The site for the new 1300-square-metre District Museum and adjacent 26-apartment residential project sits in the northwest quadrant, above West Street, the city's western arm, and the medieval cathedral.

Chichester's character changes markedly just north of West Street and its freestanding medieval bell tower. The immediate vicinity of the museum site was irrevocably altered during the 1960s and 1970s, when many of the historic buildings that once formed the street scene were swept away. Consequently, few buildings of evident architectural significance survive, beyond those listed on Tower Street to the south and opposite the museum site. The site for the museum is currently a brownfield car park, beneath which are the remains of the city's Roman baths.

In response to this setting, Williams' museum and residential project attempts to establish a new urban grain by creating a unified block with a new set of buildings along Tower Street and Woolstaplers setting up a new coherent streetscape. Planning consent was granted in January 2009 and construction will begin in early 2010.

The Roman baths, dating from the Flavian period (69–96 AD) of the Roman city Noviomagnus Regni, were discovered in the 1970s and will be displayed in situ in the entrance gallery. The baths will become an intrinsic part of the Museum, with the new galleries floating above the displayed archaeology. The building will contain permanent and temporary galleries, collection storage, workshop, research and library spaces and a learning room, in addition to public facilities.

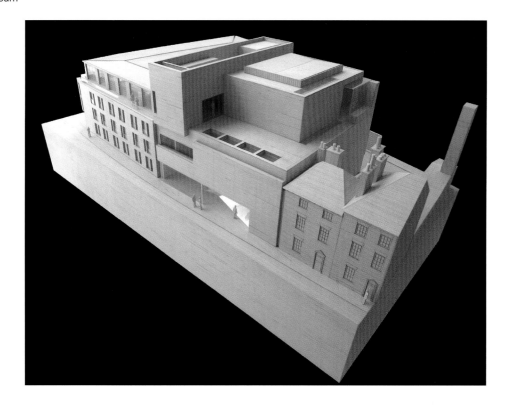

The Museum collection includes more than 1000 geological specimens (primarily fossils), some 8500 social history artefacts and items of ephemera, more than 3600 photographs and in excess of 300,000 archaeological finds describing the story of Chichester District. The new public galleries, which will exhibit key artefacts in a changing curatorial programme, are stacked vertically on three levels and linked by a processional stair culminating with views across the city to the cathedral from the building's highest level.

The city's set-piece public and religious structures such as the market cross, cathedral and bell tower are all constructed in pale stone in a city that is otherwise brick or render. The new museum will be clad in pale reconstructed stone, establishing its architectural and cultural connection with Chichester's grander public structures and creating an architectural accent among Tower Street's otherwise brick buildings. The residential development is seen as fulfilling a supporting architectural role to the museum and is composed of red brick with a set-back attic storey consistent with the typical housing model of the city.

Both the museum and the residential scheme take a three-storey parapet level consistent with the general scale of the city and the listed buildings to the south on the east side of Tower Street, while the zinc-clad residential attic storey is recessed to be read as part of the roofscape. At its northern end, the museum's main elevation incorporates a cubic turret to introduce variety and accent to the street scene and to announce the museum to both West Street and the approach from the city walls to the north.

The new museum, when realised, is intended to achieve a delicate balance between the contemporary and the historic. The museum will be a new symbol a city that is proud of its heritage but recognises that, like all cities, it must also embrace cultural change.

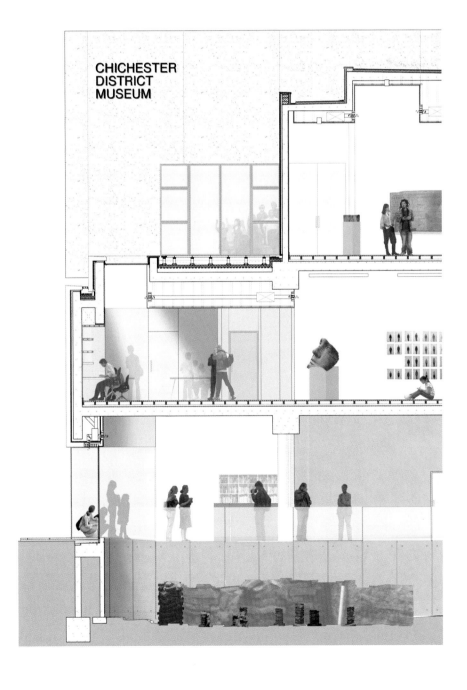

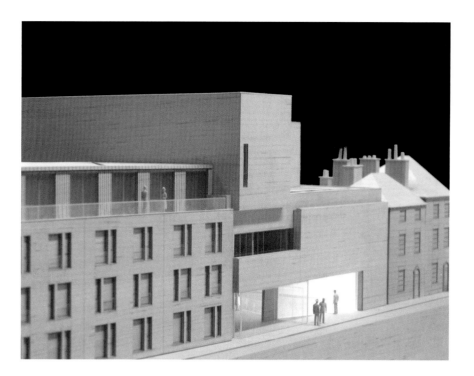

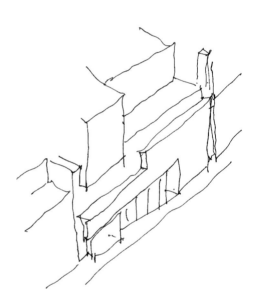

Level 2

Level 1

Ground

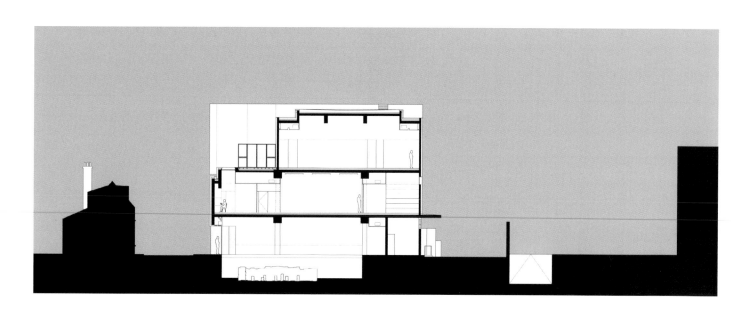

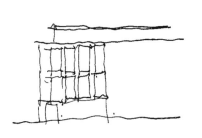

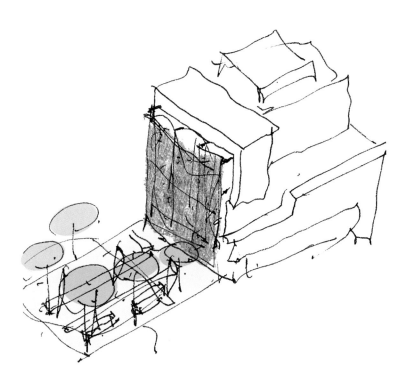

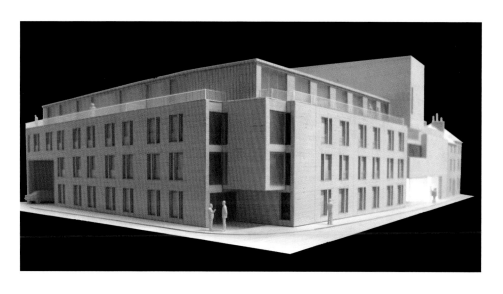

Birmingham REP and the Birmingham City Library
Birmingham, England, 1998–2007

The Birmingham Repertory Theatre first opened in 1971 and was executed in a subdued neo-brutalist style by the architect Graham Winteringham. Facing onto Centenary Square, one of the principal public spaces in the city, the REP is one of Britain's foremost theatre companies. Williams' 1999 internal remodelling was his first theatre project and the starting point for many of his ideas on theatrical spaces. The scope of the project included the complete reshaping of the 824-seat auditorium, stage and flying equipment and environmental services. The project was completed on site within a 12-week programme and opened to the public on 22 October 1999.

At the time, Williams was acutely aware that a strategic approach was needed to reorder and replan the entire building and rework its relationship with Centenary Square. He devised an overall scheme for a 13,000-square-metre redevelopment of the existing building that included, in addition to the remodelled auditorium, the provision of a new variable form 250- to 350-seat second performance space, the reorganisation of back of house facilities and a major new civic-scale front of house to re-establish the REP's urban presence within the city. That strategic project remained unexecuted.

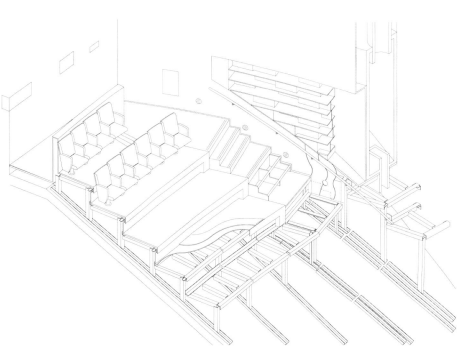

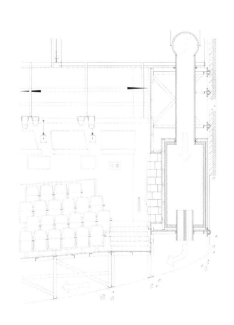

Existing Birmingham REP Theatre

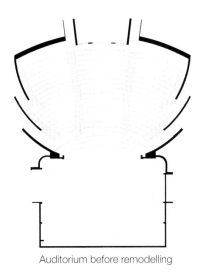

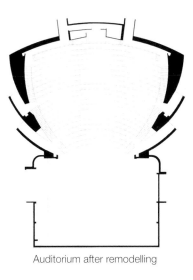

Auditorium before remodelling

Auditorium after remodelling

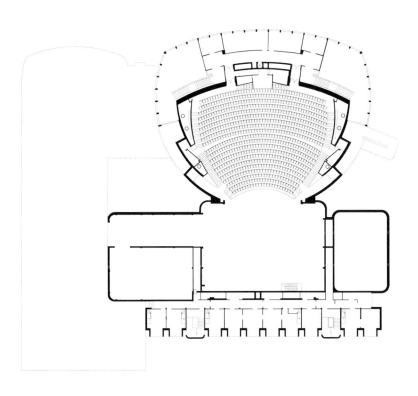

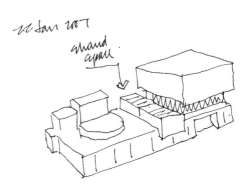

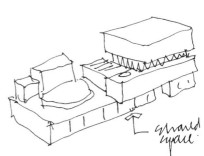

Birmingham City Library attracts approximately three million visitors per year and is currently housed in a 1970s concrete building, somewhat reminiscent of Boston's City Hall and located in the city centre, just east of Centenary Square. The independent decision by Birmingham City Council to redevelop the City Library and plan a new library building on the vacant car park site directly abutting the REP's eastern flank opened the way for a strategic masterplan to unite the two sites. In a radical project that would create the city's most important cultural complex, Williams' visionary masterplan proposed the co-joining of the new 30,000-square-metre City Library and the existing REP, on their adjacent sites.

This far-reaching strategy envisaged an interlocking of the two buildings, which not only solved a fundamental problem in that the proposed library site was too small to offer the large-scale floor plates needed for modern library use, but also offered the possibility of synergies through shared facilities between both organisations.

The proposal extensively remodelled and re-fronted the existing REP building and integrated it with the new library alongside, allowing each element to retain its distinct identity within one of Britain's most important cultural projects. In total these two buildings cover approximately 40,000 square metres.

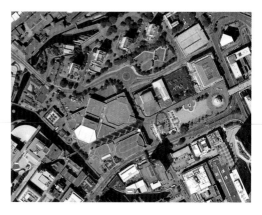

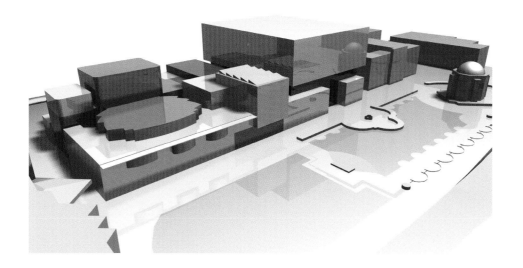

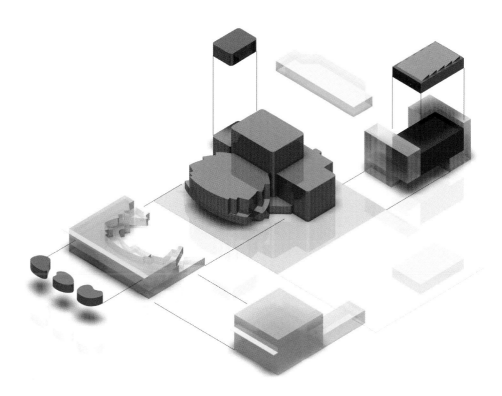

Sculpture Building, Royal College of Art
RCA Battersea Campus, London, England, 2007

A 9000-square-metre invited project for the relocation of the Fine and Applied Arts Faculties to the Royal College of Art's emerging Battersea campus, the scheme centred on the provision of student teaching and painting studios gathered around a major forum, a key social space for the college and public exhibition gallery.

The making of art is a pursuit that has traditionally occupied the twilight zones of cities, often in reclaimed industrial or warehouse buildings where the rents are cheap or non-existent and the space and light plentiful.

This area of Buttersea, appropriately a district in flux, retains a fragmented quality, with a raw, gritty atmosphere of redundant warehouses, while also being in the throes of significant development with nearby upmarket riverside apartments.

The project presented the opportunity to explore the visual identity of the RCA Battersea campus as self-evidently a creative place. Advanced in terms of its handling of its internal environment and sustainability, aesthetically Williams saw the project as both rough and raw, a clearly identifiable new building contrasting sharply with the main RCA South Kensington campus, some 3 miles distant.

Space for the making of art needs to be simple, with good light and adequate space and height in which to work. In this scheme various studios were top-lit with north light, sidelight, clerestory lighting or with transparent wall surfaces that collectively form a rich variety of spatial scale and light.

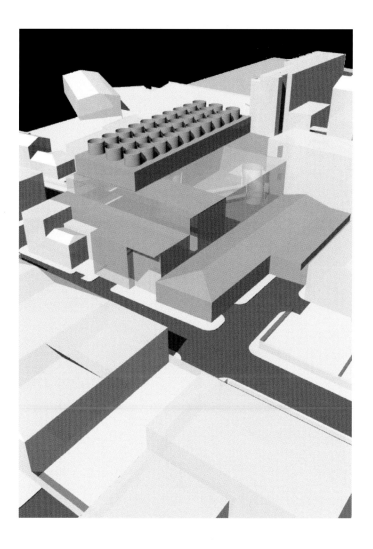

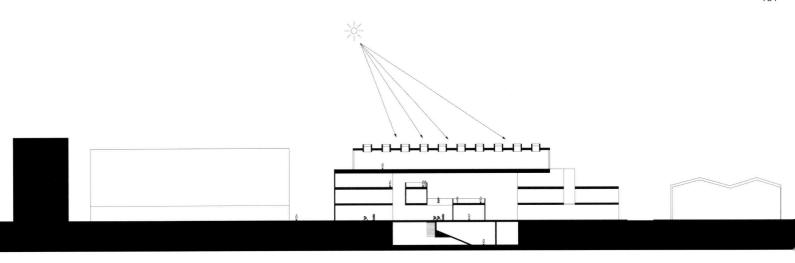

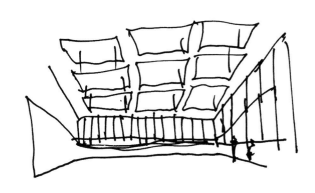

In formal terms, the project was seen as a mesa (or plateau), created by the architectural expression of the Super Studio at the top of the building. The Super Studio is derived from the concept of a re-colonised factory, large and lofty shell or receptor space with top lighting that can remain open or be readily subdivided in modular and changeable ways to create top-lit studios or cells, each of which can be readily personalised and then renewed year on year with each influx of new students. The Super Studio combines the idea of the factory warehouse with the ideal 19th-century model of a painting studio as exemplified at Mackintosh's Glasgow School of Art.

The Forum brought to the project a different, more dynamic kind of top-lit and side-lit social space on a grand urban scale. Taking the form of a large multi-level light-filled covered space containing lecture facilities, cafés, study decks and breakout pods, it was intended as the key social space for students and staff in the college, allowing direct visual connection and therefore permeability between the departments. The project was to be clad in Corten steel to emphasise the relationship with the notion of raw beauty and between art, industry and production.

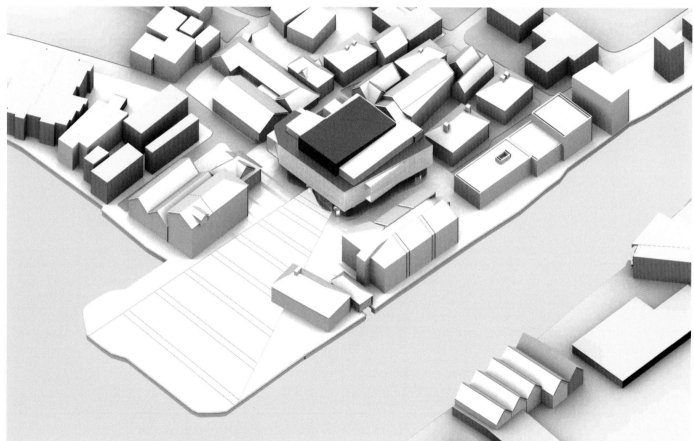

Flekkefjord Kulturhus
Flekkefjord, Norway, 2006

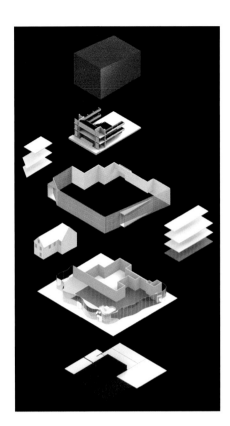

Flekkefjord is a small fishing town on the south coast of Norway, roughly equidistant between Stavanger and Kristiansand. Its traditional quarter, the site of this project, is characterised by 19th-century white clapboard timber vernacular pitched-roof buildings laid out in a close-knit street pattern. The new 4060-square-metre Flekkefjord Kulturhus contains the new town library, contemporary art galleries, a culture school, cinema, youth club and a 200-seat multiform theatre. Williams' designs for the invited competition represent a radical reinterpretation of the maritime town's vernacular architecture as a basis for composition and contextual link.

The upper part of the building design is akin to a floating crystal enwrapping the building and surmounting a transparent undulating base. The crystal upper levels house the main theatre, with the skin punctuated by clear-glazed panels giving vista and vantage onto the townscape and sea from key high-level theatre foyer and gallery areas. At the street-level base, the two-storey façade that wraps the double-height foyer, library and public spaces appears as a diaphanous curtain by day and a shimmering undulating band of light by night. The façade is intended to symbolise a new openness and a dynamic era for the socio/cultural life of Flekkefjord and its connection to the sea.

The 200-seat auditorium was designed as a flexible, adaptable space capable of being simply transformed between its multimodal states. The 4.2-metre-high galleries, which include space for both temporary and permanent exhibition, are located on two levels and provided simple, regular gallery space at the top of the building. Demountable partitions were designed to be changeable for the hanging of different types of displays, whether painting, sculpture, conceptual or digital art.

The upper levels of the building are clad in vertical-jointed glazed panels with white-coloured glass and vertical lap as a fresh interpretation of shiplap timber, which was traditionally used horizontally to clad town buildings. Internal timber screens control the amount of light and view that the building engages with, allowing the structure to be responsive to both local events and the seasons.

At ground level, the external public spaces between the new building and the sea were seen as key for festivals, extending the cultural range of activities particularly during the summer months, with the new Kulturhus conceived as the hub around which the cultural life of the region would revolve.

Careful consideration of the materiality and urbanity of the locale allowed the proposition of a dynamic, highly contemporary building, which was also respectful of Flekkefjord's special architectural and townscape qualities.

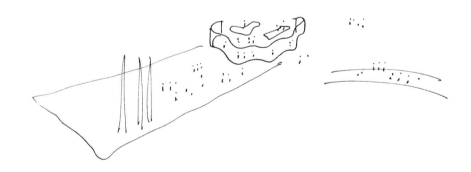

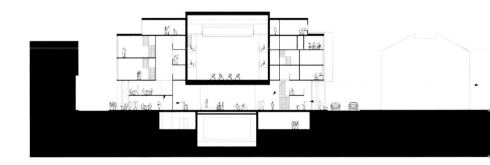

New Marlowe Theatre
Canterbury, England, 2007–2011

Named after Christopher Marlowe, Canterbury's famous Tudor playwright and contemporary of Shakespeare, the new 4850-square-metre building will replace the existing theatre on its site in Canterbury's historic core.

The Marlowe Theatre has a very large audience following and is a key part of the cultural life of Canterbury and its region. The existing theatre building, a converted 1930s cinema, seems more akin to low-grade, jazzy seaside architecture than the major theatre in one of Britain's finest historic cities. This building has now been demolished and only the steel frame structure of the existing flytower and its sub-stage remain. The new Marlowe Theatre is being built in its place on an expanded site that includes adjacent brownfield land connecting the site to the banks of the River Stour as it winds through the city centre.

The new building will contain a 1200-seat main auditorium with two curved balconies, flytower and orchestra pit, a 150-seat second space, cafés and bars as well as rehearsal and backstage facilities. The main elements will be united by an enwrapping colonnaded glazed foyer, which will connect the theatre's new public spaces and terraces to the Stour.

The building has been treated as a single composition, but one that is heavily modelled so as to rise in steps from the scales of St Peter's Church and the existing buildings along The Friars, the street on which the Marlowe sits, to the pinnacle of the remodelled flytower. An 8-metre-high reconstructed stone colonnade enwraps the glass foyer, unifying and mediating between the necessarily large components, such as the main auditorium and flytower, and the two- and three-storey historic buildings along The Friars. It also provides shelter to the south-facing foyer from solar gain.

The three-level foyer unites all the major public spaces and the two auditoria. It is seen as a crystal ribbon by day, transforming into a blade of light by night – an open and inviting place providing a new kind of meeting space within the city with the potential for extended social and cultural activity.

After the Bell Harry cathedral tower, the old Marlowe's flytower was the second tallest structure in the city. Lumpen and aesthetically crude, it contained, however, the minimum functional volume for its theatrical purpose. Williams determined that in the new project its form be remodelled to create accent and a more dynamic silhouette than a rectangular functional shape could provide. In a radical move, he proposed a new form for the flytower – some 9 metres taller at it highest point than the existing flytower – to create a pinnacle. This proposal adjacent to a World Heritage site sparked much controversy in the city, but was in the end accepted.

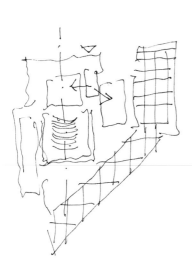

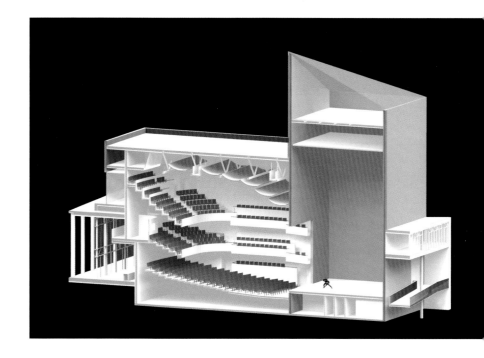

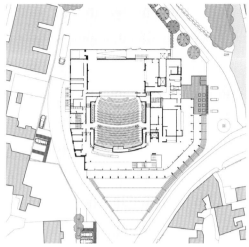

Site plan

Oriented towards the cathedral, the new flytower form may be seen as a prominent pinnacle of secular architecture within the city, while ensuring that the tower of the mediaeval cathedral's architecture retains its predominance. The flytower's surfaces will be clad in a stainless steel mesh skin set 500 millimetres in front of silver aluminium cladding. These materials are designed to dematerialise the flytower's form and cause its surfaces to shimmer and sheen while subtly reflecting clouds and the hues of the daytime sky and sunset. The flytower will be lit at night to increase the dramatic effect of the theatre both upon approach and from afar.

In a move that echoes the elevated main theatre at the Unicorn 2001–2005, the second auditorium is lifted 5.5 metres above entrance level to allow the foyer to slide beneath and maintain visual connection with the river. The second auditorium's external skin is clad in pre-oxidised copper to create a visual distinction between the two auditoria and to form a contextual connection with the red-and-brown roofscape of the city.

The scheme was granted planning permission in August 2008 and construction began in May 2009.

The former Marlowe Theatre demolished to make way for the new project

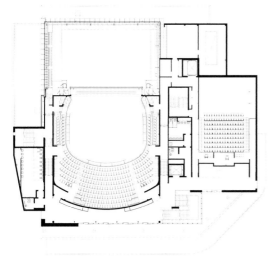

Level 3

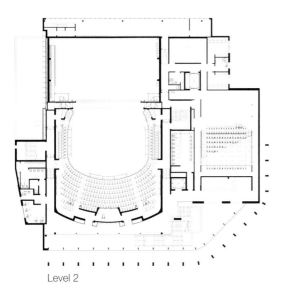

Level 2

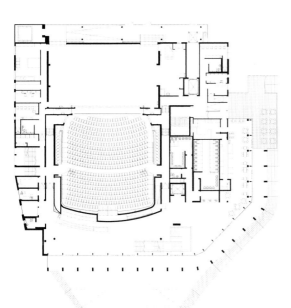

Level 1

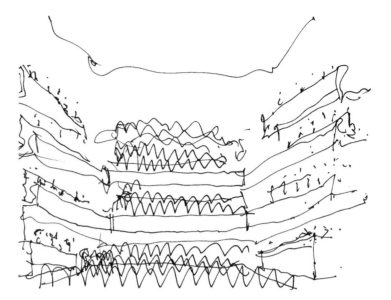

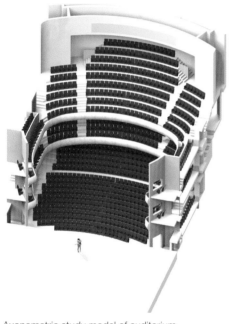

Axonometric study model of auditorium

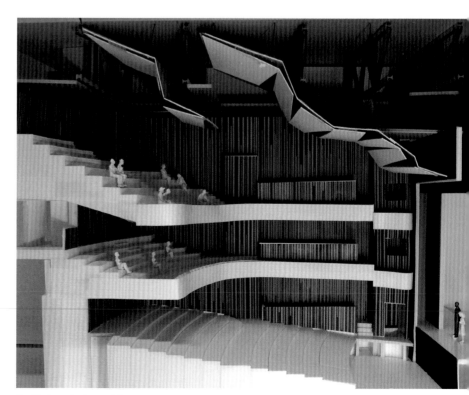

Auditorium study model

Auditorium study model

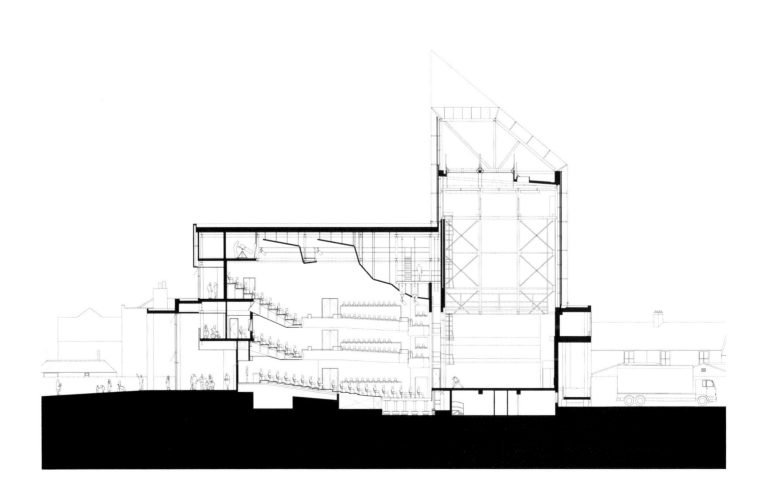

Søfartsmuseum
Helsingør, Denmark, 2007

Kronberg Castle, situated on a promontory overlooking the straights to Sweden, is a UNESCO World Heritage Site, one of only four in Denmark. The new Søfartsmuseum (Maritime Museum) is seen as a fundamental component of the cultural transformation of the Helsingør waterfront, which aims to upgrade or replace the now redundant maritime industry buildings that populated the site during the 19th and early 20th centuries.

The project's site, immediately adjacent to Kronberg Castle and its lands, was a former commercial dry dock dating from the 1950s, complete with sea gates opening direct to the harbour. The new museum was required to establish a new cultural and touristic focus of a high architectural and urban order that recognised both the World Heritage Site setting of Kronberg Castle and the character of the former industrial dockfront in transition.

The views towards Kronberg Castle were to remain unobstructed, therefore creating an essential dichotomy of visibility versus invisibility. A further design challenge was how best to signal an important new, subterranean cultural building.

Williams determined in this invited competition project that the Søfartsmuseum should be reached by a long, grand stair sliding gently down through a huge slot in a new public forecourt by the water's edge in front of the Kulturvaerft, a former industrial building being upgraded in phases as an arts centre. The descent brings the visitors to the Museum galleries at the lowest level of the former dry dock. This basic move permitted a virtually unchanged perspective towards Kronberg Castle, with only the 1.1-metre-high stone and glass guarding to the new entrance stair slot visible above ground.

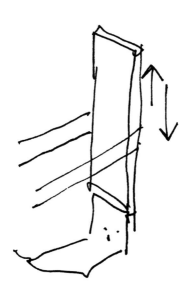

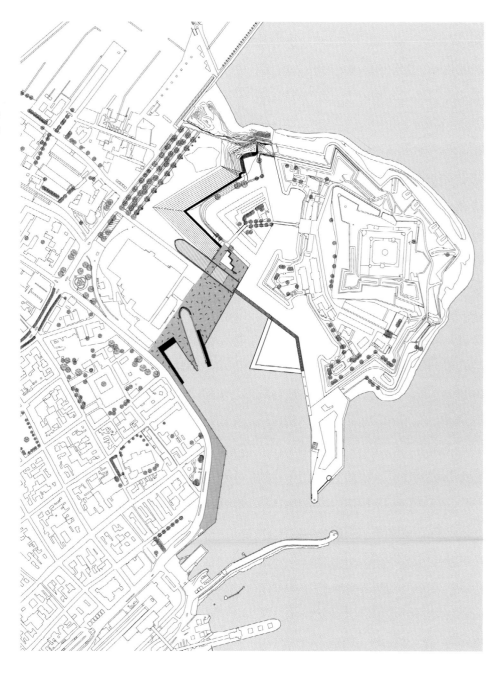

The dichotomy of visibility versus invisibility was resolved by treating kinetically the most visible architectonic component, a sliding 10-metre-high moving obelisk at its subterranean entrance that could be raised vertically up to 7 metres above ground level to mark the entrance to the museum. The gate, when open, read as an obelisk and a symbol of the museum, yet when slid away would not be apparent above forecourt level.

The dock gate could also be retracted in poor weather or high winds, thus acting as an entrance signifier and, to a certain degree, a weather barometer; its operation would be simple, using basic dock gate technology or counterweight mechanisms. The subterranean dry dock is roofed over to create the museum envelope with a partially glazed, partially solid roof, readily expressing the dock shape on plan at forecourt level. The design called for the entrance staircase and wall linings to be made of stone.

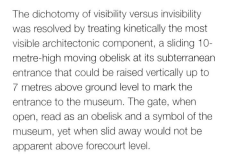

The reused dry dock forms a vast super gallery, a giant host space some 125 metres long and 25 metres wide, with a 9-metre clear internal height into which exhibits and display areas could be inserted. The proposals retain the specific character of the drained dock, complete with its textures, wear and damage, and treat all exhibits as new elements within the museum host space.

In place of the old dock gates, a large maritime window is inserted into the outside skin of the new building to give direct visual contact with the ocean, underscoring the relationship between the dock structure, the Søfartsmuseum's content and man's connection with the sea.

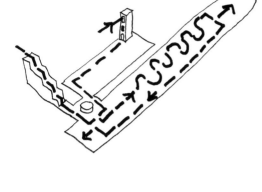

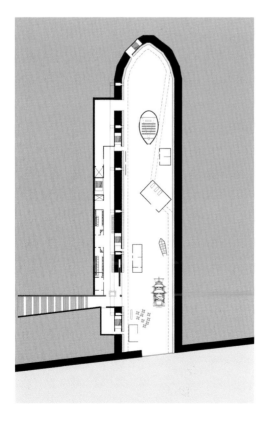

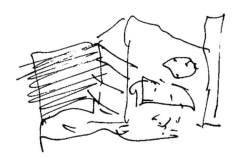

New Civic Centre
Crawley, England, 2007

Crawley is a small market town, originally dating from the 13th century, that expanded rapidly following its designation among the first wave of new towns under The New Towns Act 1946. Key organising urban spaces within the 1940s plan include Queens Square and the Boulevard, the main east–west artery on which the existing Town Hall is situated.

A strategic masterplan for the commercially led renewal of the town centre by the architects BDP included a realignment of the Boulevard and the establishment of the new site for Crawley Town Hall, off axis at the boulevard's westernmost extremity. The prominent off-axis position opened the opportunity for an asymmetrical treatment in architectural composition of the new building itself.

The new Town Hall was envisaged as a key symbol of the modern face of local government – open, accessible, both formal and informal and responsive to change and need. Incorporating a new type of public space for exchange, meeting, activity and debate, it is designed as a type of modern-day informal civic forum.

The forum – a generous, light, triple-height space beneath the office floors – was brought to the street edge and wrapped up the main façade so that the public populates the higher levels of the building. The tower and the grouping of the larger, public-use elements, such as meeting rooms and a separate 400-seat auditorium, provided architectural accent aiding the visibility of the new building when viewed along the boulevard.

Skinned in a glass façade, the activities of the building appear contained as objects within a window, with people movement on display giving animation to the entrance façade. Symbolically, therefore, both public and the executive occupy the main façade. The upper levels were developed as a dense crystalline form with solar screening controlling heat ingress, adding richness to the architectural expression of the façade.

The forum and chamber spaces allow the programming of a range of events such as cultural, musical, drama and conference, which adds a new dimension to the public perception of what a 21st-century town hall can be.

The building is intended to facilitate contact between the Council and its constituency in an open, responsive and stimulating new environment appropriate for the changing needs of society, where effective local democracy relies upon a consensual agreement between the governors and the governed.

Level 2

Level 1

Ground

Molde Theatre and Jazzhouse
Molde, Norway, 2007

Molde is a small port on the west coast of Norway. Known as the Town of the Roses, it hosts an important annual international jazz festival in the summer months, which currently operates from a small, poorly equipped theatre and a series of temporarily erected stadium-seated open venues.

The town was badly bombed during the early stages of World War II, and consequently the port's edge was completely rebuilt in a series of laminar layers or plates, echoing the profile of the waterfront and stepping up with the contour of the land. These plates contain commercial, residential and hotel buildings as well as the town's principal church and town hall. Further inland, a series of freestanding villas sits in the landscape north of Gørvellplassen, the project site, as the land rises sharply from the more gently layered coastal strips.

The invited project for Molde's new Jazzhouse presented the opportunity to establish an 8000-square-metre cultural complex incorporating a new performance space for the jazz festival and its administrative headquarters, as well as new spaces for the town's art gallery and library. Residential units, together with a series of external stepped public terraces, resolved the steep drop at the site's northern edge and completed the project's re-ordering of Molde's urban morphology.

The surrealist artist Kurt Schwitters spent time in the late 1930s residing on the island of Hjertoya, outside Molde, until the Nazis invaded Norway. His work has been a strong influence on the cultural life of the region. The Jazzhouse project takes certain cues from Schwitters' picturesque and spatial language, particularly the graphical quality of his sound poem Ursonate, which established a series of radical typographical linear patterns. These were used to inform the project's development, particularly its urban plan, which evolved into a form of urban collage made of laminar urban layers within which the programmatic elements of the project were placed.

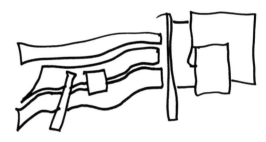

The site, Gørvellplassen, is currently an open public car park and taxi stand linked by steps to a street, Sandvegen, some 10 metres above, and is situated at the inland edge of the post-war coastal strip plan. The Jazzhouse project presented the opportunity to connect the level differences across the site to combine building, landscape and city in a coherent composition while also repairing the fragmented nature of Gørvellplassen. A new external stair connects the terraces and all public levels as well as integrating building, landscape and the new main pedestrian routes through this part of Molde.

In the proposal, the theatre and Jazzhouse were elevated to form the highest and most dominant elements in the building complex, creating a natural reference point in the town. The remaining cultural components were arranged to define the new public terraces. A new retail and residential building positioned along Sandvegen completed the upper edge of the urban block.

The auditorium is designed as a flexible, adaptable space capable of being simply transformed between its multimodal states. It provides sufficient space for 550 seated audience members or alternatively can be subdivided to allow a smaller room configuration to accommodate 200 to 250 people for jazz concerts.

The art gallery forms a small pavilion that sits on the first terrace together with the jazz museum and café, while the library and foyer define the edge between the building and the public terrace. The roof of the library forms a new, elevated terrace and repeats a pattern of similar spaces in Molde, notably the elevated square in front of the main church that doubles as the roof of City Hall.

As an experiment in materiality, the surfaces of the Jazzhouse were envisaged as printed over concrete in an abstract textural pattern derived from the structure of the rose. The Jazzhouse project was conceived as a key generator in the further development of the city, establishing a complex that provided great cultural diversity through its internal program and its span across music, the visual, literary and performing arts.

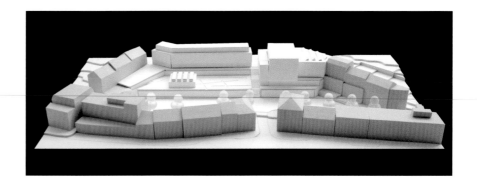

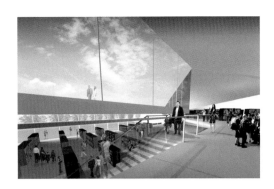

Residential Tower
81 Black Prince Road, London, England, 2007–

Black Prince Road is the Williams office's first tower project and is located near the River Thames in London's Vauxhall. The highly complex project is sandwiched between the railway viaduct into Waterloo and the tight-knit Victorian street pattern that surrounds it. The primary historical activity in the area was industry, with pottery manufacture predominating. With the subsequent decline of manufacturing in inner-city areas, substantial redevelopment of former industrial buildings and slum dwellings occurred in the 1950s.

The development site is an irregular plot that is currently occupied by a redundant, seven-storey 1950s office building. The tower will contain a total of 101 private and social sector flats, with commercial development in the base storeys. The project is affected by protected strategic views and has been carefully modelled to ensure it will make an elegant contribution to the London skyline. The building, although set back one block from the river, will offer spectacular views of the Houses of Parliament from the seventh floor and above.

The parallelogram plan combined with a vertical taper gives the building a blade-like appearance. The taper helps maximise daylight into the existing residential buildings along Salamanca Place and makes the tower appear more slender by introducing an exaggerated perspective from whichever side the building is viewed. Sitting between the riverside towers of Westminster House and the recently approved Hampton House, the building will add verticality to the silhouette of the river frontage that currently appears monolithic.

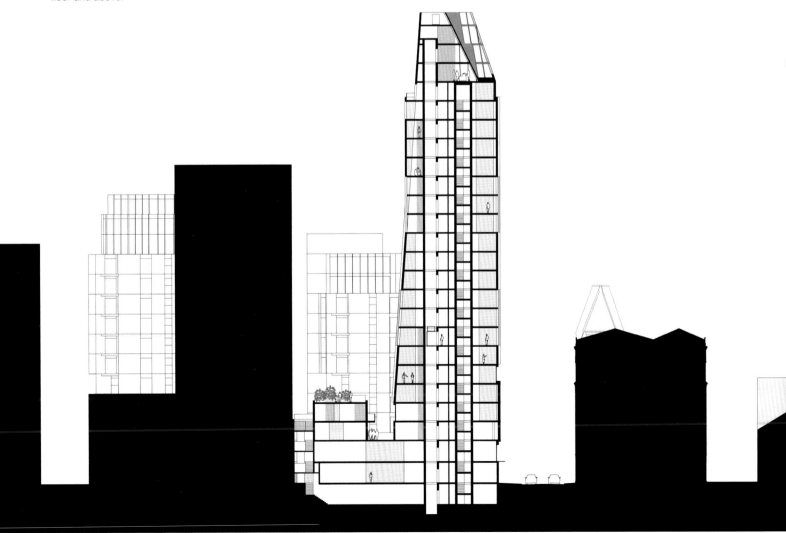

This verticality is accentuated by its fenestration, which employs slender vertically oriented window and cladding panels. The summit of the building has been sculpted into a stepped form that peaks on the riverside. The building's surfaces are solid, with punctuations for the syncopated pattern of the window openings giving a rich façade texture. At the uppermost levels, the building becomes more heavily glazed, with a crystalline element forming the junction of the building with the sky.

On plan, the tower's façades are split into two embracing plates that encapsulate the glazed body of the building. The meeting points of the two plates occur at the clipped-off corners of the parallelogram plan, where a series of cascading balconies form a 'zipper' that runs up each leading edge of the tower. At the cranked corners of the plates, stepped balconies appear as 'knuckles' to articulate these key corners. These simple devices give a clear reading of the whole building as a single object in the townscape, one that has been crafted to exploit the opportunities presented by the site's urban situation.

The floor plates in the tower repeat in groups of three and the window locations are generally the same on each of the three levels in a set, before shifting on the set above. This generates strips of tall, slender glazing panels that are dispersed in a semi-random pattern across the solid plate surfaces as an applied design. The windows themselves are detailed to read as objects formulated as part of a grander expression of the building's form. Combined into strips or stacked together, the windows are designed to be perceived as single motifs in the wider façade. The windows are proud of the plane of the wall to aid construction and to modulate the wall surfaces.

Site location

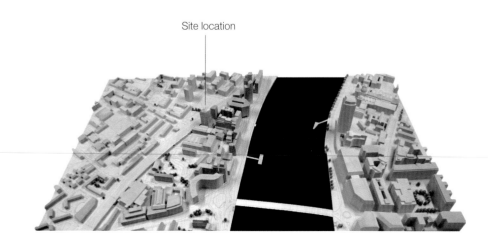

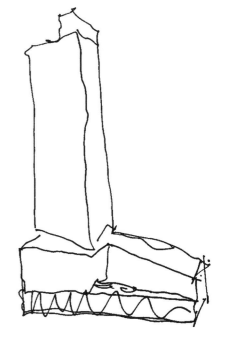

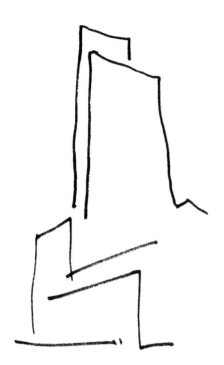

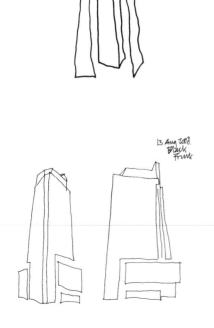

13 Aug 2008.
Black
Frame

29 FEB 2008.

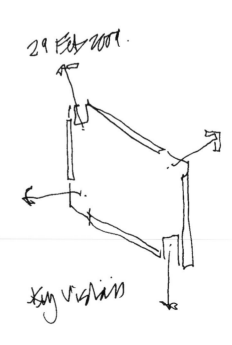

Key vistas

Concerns over the potential for overlooking into the existing habitable rooms on adjacent sites has led to a fenestration system on the podium based on three-storey angled blades of stone and glass to angle direct views along the street. The differing architectural expression clearly separates the tower from the base to allow each to be read independently.

Modern orthodoxy would suggest the tower as an entirely separate entity sitting on a podium base, with a recessed band to express the separation between them. In this case, the junction between the two has evolved so that the two elements still appear distinct from one another but are interlocked, while ensuring that the scale of the base is read as the dominant element at street level. The completed tower will offer spectacular views out to the River Thames, the Houses of Parliament, the City, Canary Wharf and the South Downs beyond.

Level 22

Level 20

Level 17

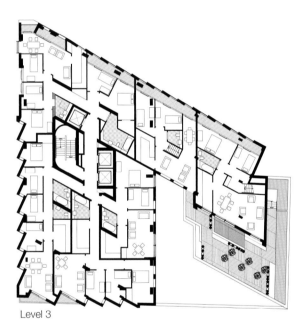

Level 3

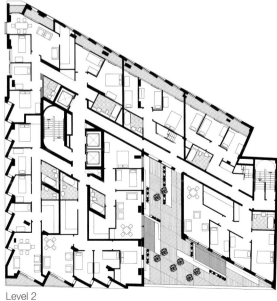

Level 2

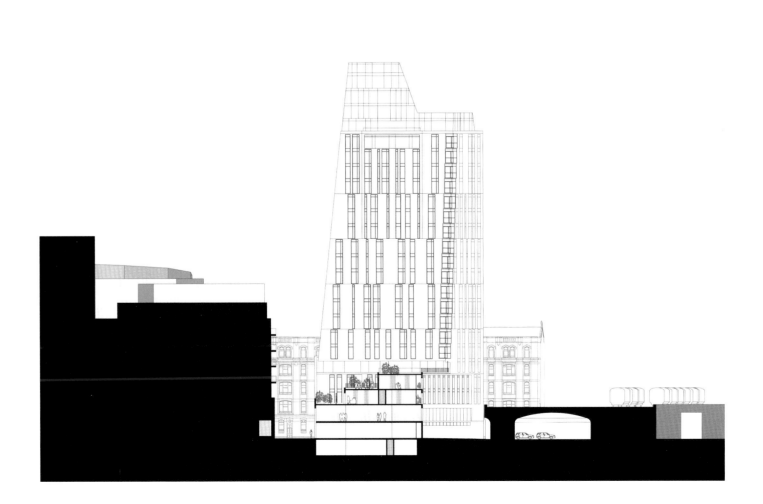

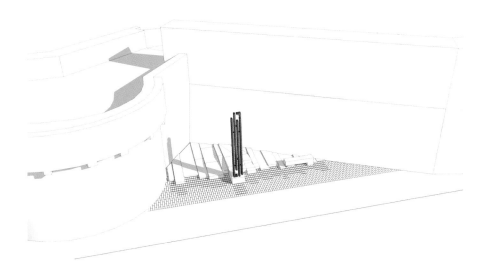

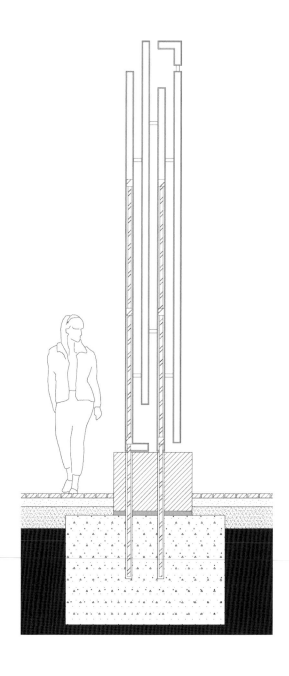

The Army Memorial
Athlone Castle, Athlone, Ireland, 2007–2009

Custume Barracks in Athlone is the headquarters of the Western Brigade. The office was asked to design a monument in Athlone close by the castle walls to honour the memory of soldiers of the Brigade who died in action, whether on peace-keeping missions abroad or while undertaking military duties at home.

The new Army Memorial is situated at the base of walls of Athlone Castle, which has its own proud military history and provides a powerful and appropriate backdrop for the new monument, which is composed of two distinct parts: the cenotaph and the plinth.

The cenotaph is the vertical element and is made from four interlocking vertical bronze plates, perhaps signifying the four compass points and implying the global spread of campaigns in which Irish men and women have fought and died. The plates are rigid and parallel, representing the enduring order, tradition and discipline of soldiery but are fractured in places to symbolise the effects of battle and war. The surfaces of the bronze will be textured.

The cenotaph is surmounted on a plinth made from Irish limestone. The plinth is constructed by a series of randomly folded stone plates, signifying the energy and movement of both youth and battle while also alluding to the diverse physical terrain in which soldiers have served and the soil on which they were raised.

The monument will be lit at night to ensure it has resonance both during the day and at night. Overall, the composition is dignified and restrained and while its contemplative abstract quality is not overtly militaristic, its monumental quality should be easily understood. The stone plinth will be inscribed in both Irish and English languages with tributes to the fallen.

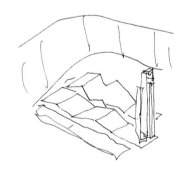

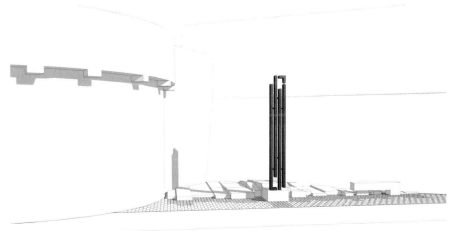

Plot 8: Former Fire Station
More London, Tooley Street, London SE1, England
2008–2011

The former fire station in Tooley Street, now
listed Grade II, was built during 1879 and
was in use until the late 1920s. It is significant
as an accomplished piece of Victorian civic
gothic revival, used efficiently and sparingly
in a new building type. Immediately adjacent
to the east is Williams' Unicorn Theatre
(2005), while to the north and west are larger
scale office buildings by Foster + Partners.

The existing building is characterised by a
U-shaped plan capped by three pitched roof
forms. The principal roof element surmounts
the main Tooley Street frontage, with the two
further roof elements running northward at a
90-degree angle, sitting above each of the
eastern and western legs of the U-shaped plan
form. The project will completely restore the
main façade and roof, rebuild the demolished
upper storey of the original watchtower and
chimney and add a series of new wings.

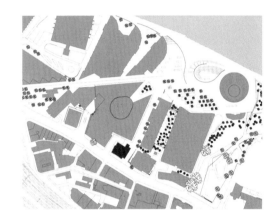

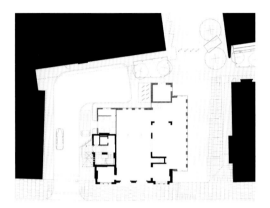

The Unicorn Theatre and the fire station may be seen in urban and conceptual terms as a pair of unequal sentinels of very different architectural styles, each contributing to the framing of the entrance to Unicorn Passage, a key pedestrian route from Tooley Street to the River Thames.

The over-arching aesthetic principle for the project is one of establishing a clear architectural legibility between the 19th- and 21st-century elements, while ensuring that the two components form a composite and balanced whole. The poor-quality post-war additions will be removed to reveal the essence of the still extant portions of the listed 19th-century building. The new wings are expressed very clearly in a simply composed, metallic anodised aluminium panel system to create a deliberate counterpoint to the ornate decorative qualities of the 19th-century neo-gothic public building.

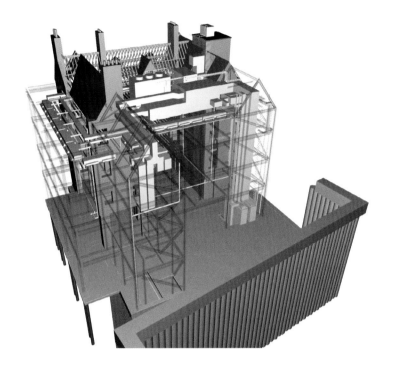

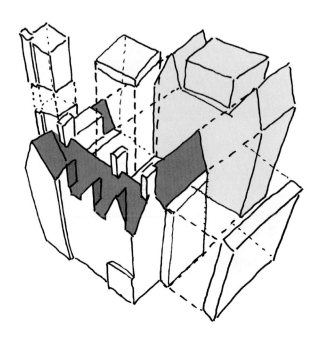

The former fire station will remain as the predominant piece in the composition, with new elements integrating its fractured northern edge with the recently constructed surrounding buildings. By extending northward and extruding the existing building's roof form with two new pitched metallic roofs and gables – together with infill sections between them and a further extension to the eastern flank – the completed development will become an asymmetrical pavilion with differing architectural treatments to each of the varying façades.

The new elevations tend to be more open and transparent to the north and east and will provide light into the heart of the plan, while the extruded pitched-roof forms are deliberately blank to their northern elevation, as they face newly built large commercial buildings immediately opposite. The composition of the new eastern and northern façades comprises a visually dense two-storey base within which the modulation is tighter, with an interstitial pilaster inserted

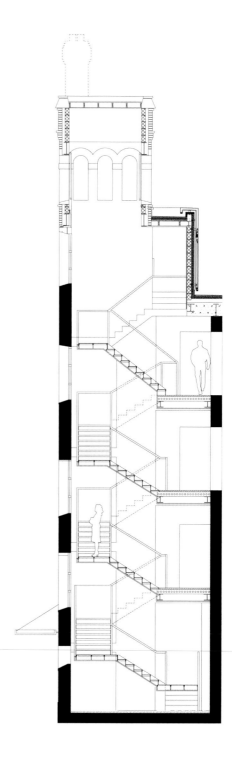

between the main guiding columnar architecture. This sets up a visual under layer that enables a higher order for the upper storeys to be introduced, thus establishing an appropriate, lighter quality. The order is deliberately interrupted at the junction between the southern façade of the new building and the southern Tooley Street elevation of the existing building. The corner pilaster will be removed to induce a greater sense of lightness as the new elements turn the Fire Station Square/Tooley Street corner and abut the flank wall.

Enwrapping that façade with new accommodation, the scheme brings life and activity – particularly at street level to complement and enhance the street life that emanates from the foyer of the Unicorn itself.

The scheme was granted planning permission in January 2009 and construction will begin in Autumn 2009.

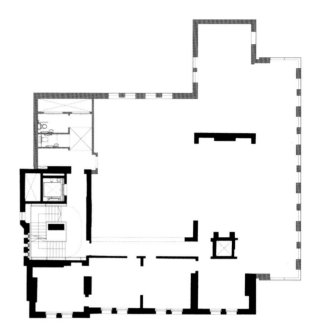

NS–Dokumentationszentrum
Munich, Germany, 2008–2009

Documentation centres – known as NS-Dokumentationszentren – have been built in Germany, notably in Berlin and Nuremburg, to establish reference points for public study and research into the Nazi period. Philosophically and conceptually, the invited Munich project is beset with the most challenging series of issues that any architect could face. The idea of an NS-Dokumentationszentrum in Munich is particularly charged in that it was this city that gave birth to Nazism, and from where it grew as a political movement to come to power in 1933.

Although one of its principal functions is display, the project is not a museum. Rather, it is a place for visitors to gain a greater understanding of the evolution, rise and consequences of the Nazi regime. The galleries will contain archive and newsreel materials but not artefacts. In addition to both temporary and permanent galleries, the building will also contain a lecture hall, library, archive, research and seminar spaces, refreshment spaces, cafeteria and staff accommodation.

The Brown House (Braunes Haus), a 19th-century villa destroyed during World War II, was the first significant building used by the Nazis as a headquarters and its former site has been chosen by the city authorities for the project. It is located on Brienner Strasse at its eastern junction with Königsplatz, the 19th-century, neo-classical square laid out by Karl von Fischer for Ludwig of Bavaria and later modified in the 20th century as a field for the mass Nazi rallies. The site is flanked by one of two surviving former Nazi administrative buildings designed for Hitler by Paul Troost, laid either side of Brienner Strasse. The northernmost building, and that nearest to the site, is now used as a theatre and music school – the Hochschule für Musik und Theater München. It faces the overgrown remains of one of the two former, so-called Temples of Honour for those killed in the 1923 Munich Putsch.

The new building is therefore situated in what was the heart of the early Nazi citadel and directly overlays the site of the first major administration centre of the regime. The preoccupying issue for Williams was the search for an appropriate architectural language, form and materiality that would create an open and transparent building that would be culturally neutral.

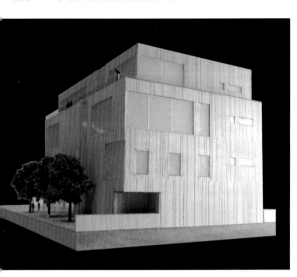
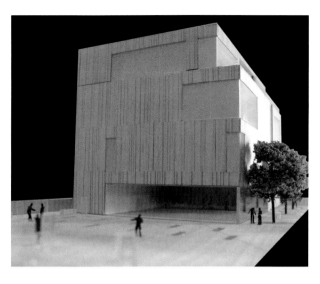

Formally, the new building has been designed as an asymmetric pavilion separated by a new forecourt from the Temple of Honour remains. The asymmetrical shifts in its composition sit counter to Troost's adjacent symmetrical, stark, 1930s neo-classical architecture and avoid any sense of the monumentality and symbolism inherent in those works. Thus, the new centre is established as a clearly independent cultural building born of a different time and political system.

At street level the foyer is glazed to provide a strong visual connection between interior and exterior, opening onto both Brienner Strasse and the new forecourt. The asymmetrical disposition of the glazing elements is used to create visual trajectories between the new building, its interior spaces and the city's key Nazi sites.

The scale, height and plan dimensions respect the urban levels and planning dimensions prescribed by the city planners. The building's upper storey is set back on Brienner Strasse and expressed in distinct materiality, and again introduces asymmetry to ensure the new architecture establishes clear cultural distance from the surrounding architecture.

The main stair rises in a top-lit void that brings light into the heart of the plan and offers a single point of reference to visitors as they move vertically through the spaces. The galleries are single spaces that are serviced and planned to allow maximum flexibility in terms of future exhibition design and layout, with each capable of displaying both object- and electronic-based exhibition forms.

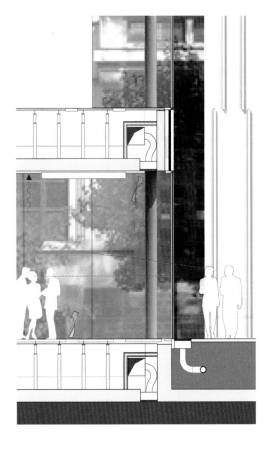

The exterior façade is clad in Muschelkalkstein (a shell-bearing limestone) laid vertically in varying width strip form with vertical, storey-height stainless steel extrusions projecting from certain joints. This stone is Munich's predominant architectural material, while the use of varying width strips introduces a subtle shifting rhythm across the façade. The introduction of stainless steel strip extrusions creates a sense of scale and a further layered cadence to the surfaces.

The landscaped forecourt breaks with the existing structure in its materiality and form. The main elements are equal rectangular blocks placed randomly either vertically or horizontally. The vertical blocks are lit and give information on the centre's activities, while flush, glazed panels in the forecourt surface bring daylight to the lower gallery and research space. The new forecourt's stone mastic asphalt surfaces are interrupted by a stainless steel strip marking the axis with Dachau, and the inherent connection between NS doctrine and its extreme implications.

Overall, the building achieves an openness and informality, which is intended to encourage a greater examination of one of the most extreme political regimes in history from the perspective of an advanced democratic society, whose forebears allowed it to happen.

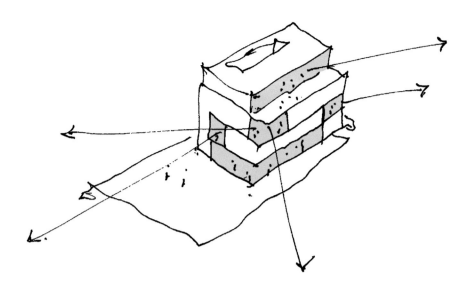

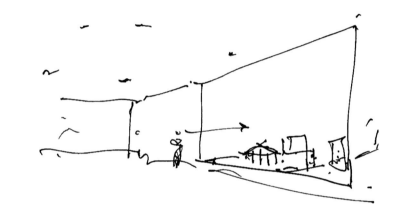

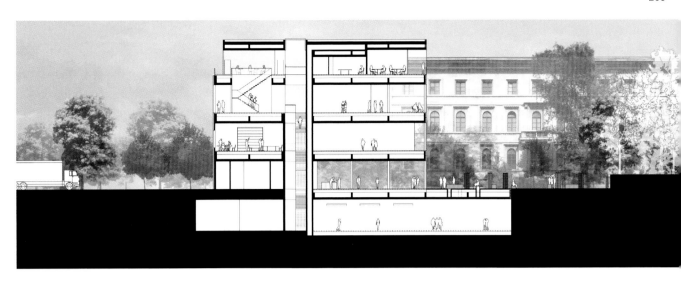

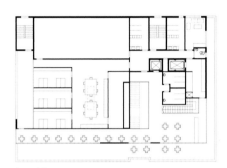

Level 3

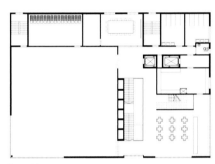

Level 2

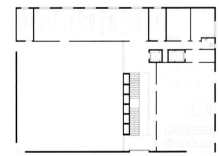

Level 1

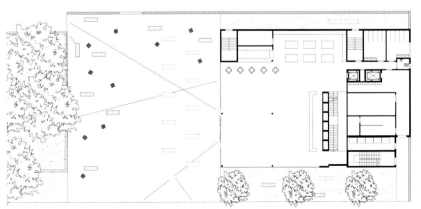

Ground floor

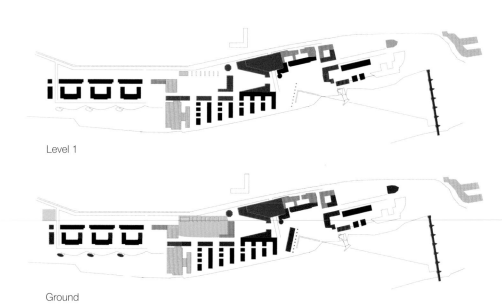

Level 1

Ground

Plaine du Pal, urban masterplan
Cahors, France

The masterplan for the Plaine du Pal sector of the historic town of Cahors in southwest France set out an urban regeneration strategy for a 2-kilometre-long strip of former industrial land alongside the River Lôt. Cahors is noted for the virtually black wine that is produced in the region and also for its medieval bridge, the three-towered Pont Valentré spanning the Lôt. The bridge is the symbol of the town and a UNESCO World Heritage site.

Historically, Cahors experienced significant development in several keys stages – the medieval period, the 16th to 18th centuries and the 19th century. Each of these stages had established a different morphology, with the medieval period being the most dense in urban terms.

Crucially, the Plaine du Pal sector, immediately downstream of the Pont Valentré, had been disconnected from the town's main core by the advent of the railway in the 19th century. The sector's land was also developed for heavy industry, which, post war, had fallen into steep decline.

Williams' response to this scenario was to create a new morphology based upon a study of the precedent building forms, heights and spaces extant within the town and to redeploy these within his new Plaine du Pal masterplan, sweeping away the redundant industrial development and creating a new coherent urban sector in its place.

The resultant masterplan establishes new links between the Plaine du Pal and the town's historic core, and also proposes a series of nodes around which particular development types and consequent activities would take place.

The nodes, principally creating cultural, touristic, residential and commercial poles, were organised according to a series of linear geometries linking one to another within a network of public spaces, culminating in a riverside linear park running directly alongside the River Lôt.

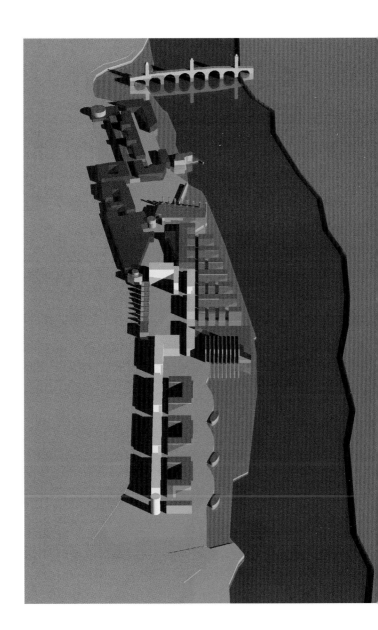

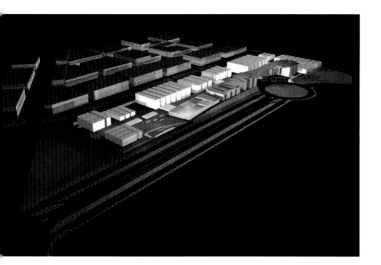

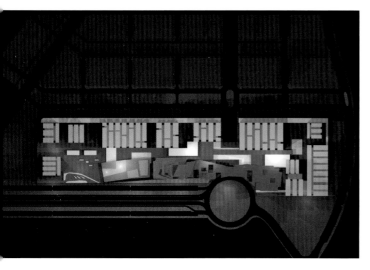

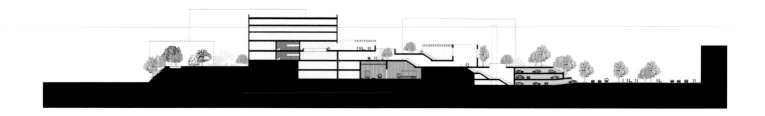

Campus de la Justicia de Madrid
Madrid, Spain, 2005

The project for the strategic masterplan for the new Madrid Law Courts and Judicial Campus comprised 14 separate law and administrative buildings totalling 300,000 square metres, on a site close to the Richard Rogers-designed Barajas airport.

The concept envisaged a landmark campus complex organised around a horizontal layering of spaces. Interconnected by courtyards and plazas on different levels, the building elements are fused into a richly ordered landscape structure providing spatial context for the judicial buildings. Each building was intended to be treated architecturally as a pavilion or palazzo, set within a coherent architectural and cityscape order. A raised dais bridging a distributor road provides a horizontal platform on which the main buildings, systems and spaces of the campus are distributed in a cohesive, united manner.

Conceptually, the campus is laid out as a cluster of buildings that takes the form of an eroded wall deployed around the western, northern, eastern and southeastern site edges. The complex was seen as a cohesive whole united by the geometry of the landscaped spaces between the buildings. Diverse precedents for this concept include the Getty Museum, Los Angeles, while earlier spatial models reference Trinity College, Dublin, Lincoln's Inn and Middle and Inner Temples in London. Each is organised around a rich sequence of spaces, which aid functionality and interconnectedness while also balancing formality and asymmetry to create a distinct identity.

Exploiting the gradient of the roads and topography, the upper surface of the dais steps down in three stages from its connection with the rail transit station to the west to the grouping of the Civil/Mercantil, Audiencia Provincial and Fiscalia buildings in the secure areas to the east. This establishes a series of linked urban spaces, creates a richly defined urban grain and avoids an alienating grand axiality on the 1-kilometre-long site.

The 14 buildings and spaces that form the campus are arranged according to the criticality of functional interrelationships, their interface with the public, security and the emblematic status within the campus hierarchy. Parking, subterranean secure systems and a vehicle service are located within the dais, enabling the complex of buildings to be fully staffed and serviced from below.

The three buildings – the Audiencia Provincial, the Tribunal Superior de Justicia and the Bloque Institucional/Decanato – form an arc on plan and are expressively composed both in urban organisation and in terms of their individual architectural expression. Acknowledging their special status within the hierarchy of the judicial system, the buildings are situated in the most visible positions in the masterplan.

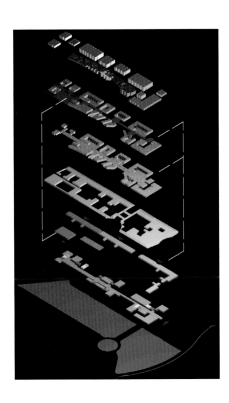

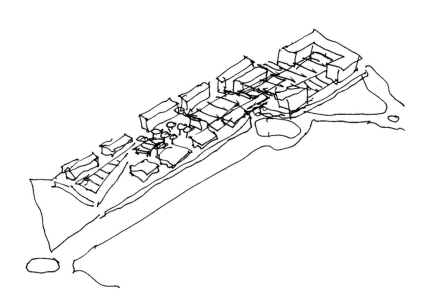

Wembley missing
link
19 March 2001

Wembley 'Missing Link' Masterplan
London, England, 2008–

Wembley, a fragmented suburb of northwest London, is in a state of transformation. The Wembley Stadium sector in the east is famous as the site of the interwar Empire Exhibition and the original national football stadium, which was recently rebuilt by Foster + Partners and HOK Sport.

The new stadium dominates the surrounding district and forms the centrepiece of a new masterplan by Richard Rogers. To the west is Wembley Central, a traditional suburban shopping district centred around Wembley Central Station, which is in the process of redevelopedment. Wembley High Road connects these two sectors, and throughout its central section is characterised by a fractured streetscape, remnants of shopping terraces from the 1930s and a series of 1960s and 1970s office buildings of different heights and scales.

To the northern side of the High Road is a large, linear parcel of railway embankment land bisected by the east–west Chiltern railway line, giving onto sharply sloping woodland to the north. Development abutting the railway cutting consists primarily of garaging, low-grade workshops and backlands that are largely isolated from the High Road. The High Road frontage itself is characterised by a largely unbroken, linear shopping strip.

Williams' masterplan for this 500-metre-long section of the High Road, colloquially known as the 'Missing Link', will connect the Wembley Central and Wembley Stadium sectors. It sets out a long-term strategy for the transformation and integration of this sector with the two eastern and western sectors, at the same time crossing the railway with garden bridges, releasing the formerly landlocked parcels against the railway for development and making crucial north–south connections. The existing White Horse footbridge marks the transition to the Wembley Stadium sector, and a series of alternate morphologies were explored to establish the most appropriate formal connections.

The sloped woodland north of the railway was categorised in the masterplan as a green parkway, a place for the enjoyment of people in an otherwise relentlessly traffic-dominated, suburban high street environment. The scheme introduced the concept of a market square at approximately midpoint along the sector, where a new 'garden bridge' would span the railway, adding urban focus at both spatial and social levels. Taller buildings at either end of the sector and adjacent to the market square give accent and focus to the proposal and intensify the development opportunities, while also marking the eastern and western approaches.

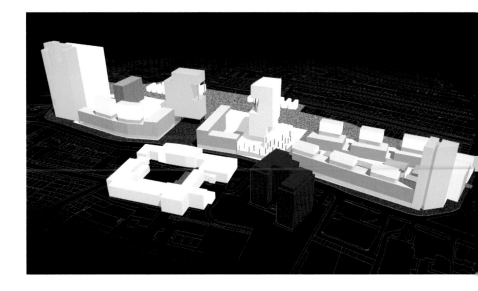

The Inside: Furniture, Fit out and Material

The way in which the Williams studio considers its buildings forces them to be treated holistically in terms of their materiality and form. The objective is always to try to get some sense of interconnection between the form and surfaces as the building textures move from the exterior to the interior.

In The Long House, Pietro Lauro limestone, which has a very consistent, slightly velvety quality when viewed in certain lights, was used for both the exterior terracing and also for the more tactile areas such as the basins, showers and floors in the bathrooms. The textures seem to create a sparse sumptuousness when taken to fine detail.

In the Athlone Civic Centre, the special surfaces such as the lining to the council chamber were executed in Black American Walnut, which has become one of Williams' favourite materials and has been used in many ways on subsequent projects to describe both surface and form. At the Wexford Opera House, where this texture clads every surface of the auditorium, the material's totality reinforces the singularity of the formal proposition while being a delight to touch.

At Athlone, the concrete coffers to the chamber weigh heavily above the space echoing the brise soleils externally, while the specially commissioned bespoke council table absorbs something of both the wall and balcony textures and the Eames high-back Soft Pad chairs that surround it.

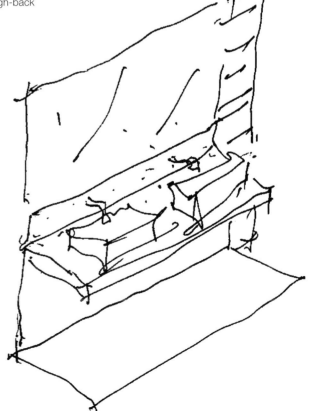

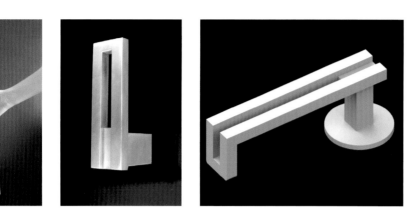

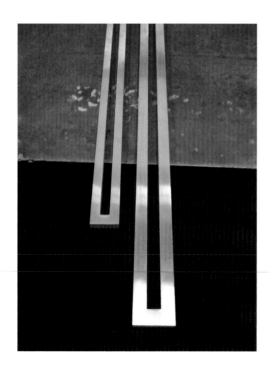

Product: Ironmongery, The Parallel Range
2004

Williams first had the opportunity to consider how to design an ironmongery range while working on Athlone Civic Centre. The joy of that project was that the client, Athlone Town Council, gave a free hand to design so many aspects of the project from the urban masterplan, the building itself, the public spaces and external seating right through to the internal door furniture.

The inspiration for the ironmongery was drawn from the linearity of the architecture, the ribbed nature of the principal façade and the trabeated concrete soffits to the library and council chamber.

The door furniture, dubbed The Parallel Range, was developed around a pair of square section parallel stainless steel bars of varying dimension dependent upon application. A motif of a bar wrapping back on itself through 180 degrees was created to make a scalable module that could form the lever furniture, the ends of the pull handles and when downscaled could also form a single coat hook.

The concepts were prototyped with specialist ironmongery manufacturer Izé Ltd in the UK. Following several physical refinements undertaken at prototype stage, final fabrication specification was arrived at. The patented range is now in production and has been used on a number of the firm's projects.

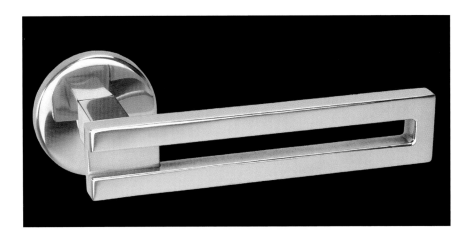

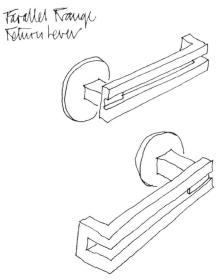

Parallel Range
Return lever

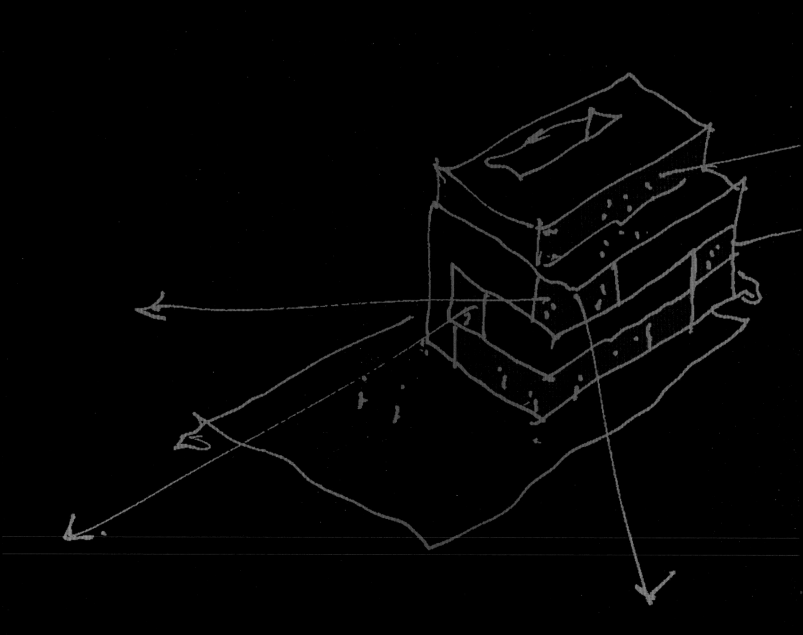

Clients

Principal clients

Athlone Town Council, Republic of Ireland

Birmingham Repertory Theatre

London Borough of Brent

Canterbury City Council

Carlisle City Council

Central Middlesex NHS Trust

Chichester District Council

Chrysalis Group plc

Comune di Torino, Italy

Devon County Council

Farnborough Air Sciences Trust

Flekkefjord Kommune, Flekkefjord, Norway

Handels- og Søfartsmuseet,
Helsingor, Denmark

Herning Art Museum, Denmark

The Highland Council

ISG Jackson

Kent County Council

Kettering Borough Council

Landeshauptstadt München, Germany

Moesgärd Museum, Denmark

Molde Kommune, Molde, Norway

Monaghan County Council,
Republic of Ireland

More London Developments

NAMCO

Natural History Museum, London

Network Housing

OPW (Office of Public Works),
Republic of Ireland

The Orange Tree Theatre, Richmond

Park & Dare Theatre, Treorchi, Wales

Rhondda-Cynon-Taf County Borough Council

Ritterman Holdings Ltd

Ristoia Ltd

Royal College of Art, London

La Sémarg, Paris, France

Shetland Islands Council

Teignmouth Community College, Devon

Tunbridge Wells Borough Council

TU Darmstadt, Germany

Unicorn Theatre, London

Various private clients

Ville de Cahors, France

West Sussex County Council

Westmeath County Council,
Republic of Ireland

Wexford Festival Opera, Republic of Ireland

Arts Clients

Birmingham Repertory Theatre

Chichester District Museum

Flekkefjord Kommune, Flekkefjord, Norway

Handels- og Søfartsmuseet,
Helsingor, Denmark

Herning Art Museum, Denmark

Moesgård Museum, Denmark

Marlowe Theatre, Canterbury

Molde Jazz Centre, Molde, Norway

Natural History Museum, London

The Orange Tree Theatre, Richmond

Park & Dare Theatre, Treorchi, Wales

Unicorn Theatre, London

Wexford Festival Opera, Republic of Ireland

Government and Local Authority

Athlone Town Council, Republic of Ireland

London Borough of Brent

Canterbury City Council

Carlisle City Council

Chichester District Council

Comune di Torino, Italy

Devon County Council

The Highland Council

Kent County Council

Kettering Borough Council

Landeshauptstadt München, Germany

Molde Kommune, Molde, Norway

Monaghan County Council,
Republic of Ireland

OPW (Office of Public Works),
Republic of Ireland

Rhondda-Cynon-Taff County Borough Council

La Sémarg, Paris, France

Shetland Islands Council

Tunbridge Wells Borough Council

Ville de Cahors, France

West Sussex County Council

Westmeath County Council,
Republic of Ireland

Health

Central Middlesex NHS Trust

Housing

Network Housing Group

Media

Chrysalis Group plc

Commercial & Development

More London Developments

NAMCO

Ritterman Holdings Ltd

Ristoia Ltd (Ireland)

Universities & Higher Education

Anglia Ruskin University, Essex

Royal College of Art, London

Teignmouth Community College, Devon

Technischen Universität Darmstadt, Germany

Various private clients

Principal architectural exhibitions

2009 Chicago Athenaeum: International Award Winners, January–February,
European Centre for Architecture Art Design and Urban Studies, Athens

2008 Chicago Athenaeum: International Award Winners, 30 October–18 November,
SESV Santa Verdiana, Faculty of Architecture, University of Florence

2008 Unicorn Theatre, National Theatre, London

2007 Royal Academy Summer Exhibition, Royal Academy, London

2007 Society of British Theatre Technicians, Victoria & Albert Museum, London

2006 RIAI Exhibition: Award Winners, Dublin

2006 Chicago Athenaeum: Award Winners, Dublin, 17 November 2006–10 January 2007, Dublin

2005 RIAI Exhibition: Award winners, Dublin

2005 RIBA Urban Space Exhibition, GLA, London

2004 Royal Academy Summer Exhibition, Royal Academy, London

2003 Unicorn Theatre, Theatre Museum, London

2003 AR MIPIM Awards, Cannes

2002 2D/3D Exhibition, Galeria Centralis, Budapest

2002 Royal Academy Summer Exhibition, Royal Academy, London

2002 2D/3D Exhibition, Sheffield Galleries

2001 Centro Culturale di Torino, Cavallerizza Reale, Turin

2001 Royal Academy Summer Exhibition, Royal Academy, London

2001 Doncaster NPV Competition, Cube Gallery, Manchester

2000 RIBA: Anglia University Competition, RIBA, London

2000 Royal Scottish Academy Summer Exhibition, Royal Scottish Academy, Edinburgh

1999 Royal Academy Summer Exhibition, Royal Academy, London

1998 Royal Academy Summer Exhibition, Royal Academy, London

1998 Four Stories, Architecture Centres: Bristol & Newcastle

1997 Royal Academy Summer Exhibition, Royal Academy, London

1996 Royal Academy Summer Exhibition, Royal Academy, London

1996 RIBA: Architecture Tomorrow, RIBA, London

1995 Royal Academy Summer Exhibition, Royal Academy, London

1993 Royal Academy Summer Exhibition, Royal Academy, London

1992 Royal Academy Summer Exhibition, Royal Academy, London

1991 Royal Academy Summer Exhibition, Royal Academy, London

1990 Tokyo International Forum Exhibition, Imagination Gallery, London

1990 Walking on Glass Solo Exhibition, Blanc de Bierges Gallery, London and
University of Edinburgh

1989 Los Angeles Urban Competition Prize Winners, Los Angeles City Hall

1988 RIBA/Ibstock '40 Under Forty' Exhibition, RIBA, London

Selected bibliography

'The Long House', *Contemporary House Design*, May 2009, pp. 200–209.

'Opera House in Wexford', *DETAIL: Musik und Theatr*, Institut für international Architektur-Dokumentation, March 2009, pp. 184–185.

Who's Who 2009, A & C Black Publishers Ltd, December 2008, Keith Williams personal biography, p. 2515.

'Virtuoso Performance', *Irish Arts Review*, Irish Arts Review Ltd, Vol. 25 No. 4, Winter 2008, pp. 122–125.

'Wexford Opera House', *Architects Journal*, October 2008, front cover and pp. 26–33 and 35.

'The House that Wexford Built', *Sunday Times*, 26 October 2008, p. 37.

'Opera 2: Wexford Winner', *The Spectator*, 25 October 2008, pp. 57–58.

'Hearts and Ice Melt in New Opera House: Wexford Opera House', *The Times*, 20 October 2008, p. 18.

'A New Era for Opera in Ireland', *The Daily Telegraph*, 20 October 2008, p. 26.

'Well in Tune: Wexford Opera House', *Financial Times: Life & Arts*, 19 October 2008, p. 14.

'Breathing Life into Grand Old Opera', *Irish Independent*, 15 October 2008, p. 15.

'Upfront: No Prima Donna', *RIBA Journal*, October 2008, pp. 8–9.

'Keith Williams Architects: Unicorn Theatre 2005', *London 2000+ New Architecture*, October 2008, pp. 158–161.

'Inside Wexford's Giant Cello', *Irish Times*, 16 September 2008, p. 16.

'The Long House, Athlone Civic Centre, Unicorn Theatre', *100 x 400 Volume 2*, July 2008, pp. 567–573.

'The Long House', *DETAIL CHINA*, June 2008, pp. 241–246.

'The Long House', *DalCasa*, Izdavac, June 2008, pp. 92–97.

'The Long House, London', *Architecture Ireland*, March 2008, pp. 13 and 38–43.

'Kultursenter in Flekkefjord, Norway', *Plan Magazine (Ireland): Architectural Review 2008*, January 2008, pp. 28–29.

Who's Who 2008, A & C Black Publishers Ltd, Keith Williams personal biography, December 2007, p. 2497.

'Secret Garden: The Long House', *HOUSE*, Autumn 2007, pp. 38–44.

'Unicorn Theatre: Winner UK Copper Awards', *Architectural Review*, October 2007, pp. 102–103.

'Inspired by the Mews: The Long House', *Architecture Today*, September 2007 (AT176), pp. 38–47.

'The New Civic Centre, Athlone', *L Industria Italiana del Cemento*, No. 832, June 2007, pp. 392–399.

'Unicorn Theatre', *New London Architecture 2*, May 2007, pp. 70–72.

'Unicorn Theatre', *Architecture & Design London*, March 2007, pp. 136–145.

'Unicorn Theatre', *Performing Architecture*, February 2007, pp. 140–143.

'Unicorn Theatre', *Architecture & Detail*, No. 66 January 2007, pp. 217–223.

'Athlone Civic Centre', *Architecture & Detail*, No. 66, January 2007, pp. 230–233.

'Unicorn Theatre', *RUM DENMARK*, November 2006, pp. 4 and 86–93.

'Theatre Beyond Child's Play: Unicorn Theatre', *AD Architectural Design*, June 2006, pp. 118–121.

'Unicorn Theatre', *Architecture Ireland*, April 2006, pp. 16–22.

'Kunstenshus Herning', *Architecture & Concept*, No. 084, April 2006, pp. 28–31.

'Ireland's Civic Pride', *A10*, March 2006, pp. 58–59.

'Civic Duty Athlone Civic Centre, Ireland', *Hinge Magazine (Hong Kong)*, Vol. 128, March 2006, pp. 60–61.

'Scene Stealer: Unicorn Theatre', *RIBA Journal*, January 2006, front cover and pp. 28–36.

'Keith Williams: Newcomer of the Year 2005', *The Daily Telegraph: Review 2005*, 24 December 2005, p. 8.

'Unicorn Theatre', *The Independent*, 7 December 2005, p. 48.

'It's Child's Play: Unicorn Theatre', *The Observer*, 4 December 2005, p. 10.

'Keith Williams/Unicorn Theatre', *Architects Journal*, 1 December 2005, front cover and pp. 23–37.

'Out with Garish Blobs, in with Glass and Glamour – Unicorn Theatre', *The Daily Telegraph*, 30 November 2005, p. 29.

'Kunstens Hus Herning', *International, Indubudt Projektkonkurrence*, November 2005, pp. 18–19.

'Contextualism zonder sentiment: Athlone Civic Centre', *de Architect*, June 2005, pp. 48–53.

'Civic Duty Athlone Civic Centre, Ireland', *Hinge Magazine (Hong Kong)*, June 2005, vol. 118, pp. 82–83.

'Athlone Civic Centre', *L'ARCA2*, L'Arca No. 202, May 2005, p. 90.

'Athlone's New Civic Centre', *Architecture & Concept*, No. 72, April 2005, front cover and pp. 21–33.

'Athlone Civic Centre', *Architecture Ireland*, February 2005, pp. 36–40.

'Irish Identity: Athlone Civic Centre', *Architectural Review*, January 2005, pp. 48–53.

Kenneth Powell, *City Reborn: Architecture & Regeneration in London*, pp. 108–109.

'Unicorn Theatre', *Arkitektur + Wettbewerb*, No. 194, June 2003, pp. 66–67.

'Unicorn Theatre for Children', *Hinge Magazine (Hong Kong)*, Vol. 94, February 2003, p. 26.

'Keith Williams adds to Athlone s Civic Stock', *Architects Journal*, 7 November 2002, p. 10.

'The Unicorn – From Myth To Reality', *The Times*, 2 May 2002, p. 38.

'Culture Center in Turin, Italia', *Architecture & Concept*, No. 31, October 2001, pp. 46–49.

'Civic Pride Drives KWA Regeneration Scheme', *Architects Journal*, 14 June 2001, pp. 6–7.

Staff and contributors, 2001–2009

Licia de Angelis

Rebecca Angus

Ilex Beinemeier

Sandra Beyer

Sascha Bischoff

Nick Bradley

Claire Brewster

Richard Brown: Director

Stephen Clarke

Cheah Yit Eet

Abigail Dalling

Bronwen Davies

Guy Davies

James Davies

Sandra Denicke

Nicola Fox

Annika Grafweg

Matthew Green

Justin Holland

Fritz Hover

Fiona Johnstone

Hanan Kandili

Sofia Kapsalis

Dan Lobato

Philipp Macke

Britta Neffgen

Michael Nettleship

Sieglinde Neyer

Bruno Paolucci

Michael Rabe

David Russell

Melanie Schubert

Clayton Shortall

Ingrid Slettern

Ludwig Steyl

Johann Strauss

Tabitha Sudbury

Mark Taylor

Mai Torvitsdam

Carl Trenfield

Thorsten Werner

Michelle Wong

Chiu Wei-Yang

Consultants

John Ahern

Graham Bizley

Vanessa Shrimpton

Martin Williams

Models

A Models

Jackie Hands

Hidden Modelshop

Kandor

Photographs

Hélène Binet

David Gandorge

Ros Kavanagh

Ger Lawler

Eamonn O'Mahony

Keith Williams Architects

Pat Redmond

Project credits

Centre Regional de la Musique et de la Voix (CRMV)
Client: La Sémarg: Argenteuil, France
Architect: Keith Williams
Acoustician: ARUP Acoustics
Theatre Consultant: Theatre Projects Consultants
Structural Engineer: ARUP
Services Engineer: ARUP
Cost Consultant: Bucknall Austin Associés
Aerial Photography: aeroGRID® Aerodata Surveys®

The MERCAT Centre
Client: The Highland Council
Architect: Keith Williams, Richard Brown
Acoustician: Sandy Brown Associates
Theatre Consultant: Theatre Projects Consultants
Structural Engineer: ARUP
Services Engineer: ARUP
Cost Consultant: Bucknall Austin Associés
Models: Jackie Hands
Photographer: Eamonn O'Mahony

Centre for Business Management and Postgraduate Studies, Anglia Ruskin University
Client: Anglia Ruskin University
Architect: Keith Williams, Richard Brown
Structural Engineer: Buro Happold
Services Engineer: Buro Happold

Rehearsal Building, Orange Tree Theatre
Client: Orange Tree Theatre
Architect: Keith Williams Architects
Keith Williams, Richard Brown, Sofia Kapsalis (project architect), Carl Trenfield, Chiu Wei-Yang
Structural Engineer: Barton Engineers
Cost Consultant: Wheelers (Concept Scheme only)
Contractor: Exel Construction Ltd.
Models: Jackie Hands
Photographers: Eamonn O'Mahony, David Grandorge
Aerial Photography: Promap® Landmark Information Group

Centro Culturale di Torino
Client: Citta di Torino
Architect: Keith Williams Architects
Keith Williams, Richard Brown, Sieglinde Neyer, Johann Strauss
Structural Engineering: Buro Happold
M & E Engineering: Buro Happold
Cost Consultant: Davis Langdon
Models: Jackie Hands
Digital Imaging: Keith Williams Architects
Photographer: Eamonn O'Mahony

The Long House
Client: Private
Architect: Keith Williams Architects
Keith Williams, Richard Brown, David Russell (project architect) Sandra Denicke, Carl Trenfield, James Davies
Planning Consultant: Turley Associates
Structural Engineer: Techniker
Quantity Surveyor: Michael F Edwards & Associates
Main Contractor: Durkan Pudelek Limited
Photographer: Hélène Binet

Athlone Civic Centre
Client: Athlone Town Council and Westmeath County Council
Architect: Keith Williams Architects
Keith Williams, Richard Brown (director in charge), Nick Bradley, Sieglinde Neyer, David Russell, Melanie Schubert
Structural Engineering: ARUP Consulting Engineers
M & E Engineering: ARUP Consulting Engineers
Façade Engineering: Buro Happold
Fire Engineering: ARUP Fire Services
Lighting Consultants: Sutton Vane Associates
Quantity Surveyor: Davis Langdon PKS
Main Contractor: John Sisk and Sons Ltd
Models: Jackie Hands
Photographer: Eamonn O'Mahony

The Unicorn Theatre
Client: Unicorn Theatre
Architect: Keith Williams Architects
Keith Williams, Richard Brown, Sofia Kapsalis (project architect), Rebecca Angus, Nick Bradley, Guy Davies, Annika Grafweg, Bruno Paolucci, Melanie Schubert, Carl Trenfield
Theatre Consultants: Theatre Projects Consultants/CharcoalBlue
Access Consultant: Buro Happold
Structural Engineering: ARUP
M & E Engineering: ARUP
Façade Engineering Concept: ARUP
Acoustician: Arup Acoustics
Cost Consultant: Bucknall Austin
Main Contractor: Mansell Construction Services
Artists: David Cotterrell, Martin Richman
Models: Jackie Hands
Photographer: Hélène Binet

Literaturmuseum der Moderne
Client: Deutches Literaturarchiv Marbach
Architect: Keith Williams Architects
Keith Williams, Richard Brown, Annika Grafweg, Sieglinde Neyer, Johann Strauss, Chiu Wei-Yang
Digital Imaging: Keith Williams Architects

Nietzsche Archive
Client: Naumburg Stadt
Architect: Keith Williams Architects
Keith Williams, Richard Brown, Nick Bradley, Sieglinde Neyer, David Russell
Digital Imaging: Keith Williams Architects

Parc & Dare Theatre and Arts Centre
Client: Rhondda-Cynon-Taf County Borough Council
Architect: Keith Williams Architects
Keith Williams, Richard Brown
Arts Consultant: DCA
Structural Engineer: Buro Happold
Services Engineer: Buro Happold
Cost Consultant: Chandler KBS
Digital Imaging: Keith Williams Architects

Irish World Music Centre (IWMC)
Client: University of Limerick
Architect: Keith Williams Architects
Keith Williams, Richard Brown, Carl Trenfield
Digital Imaging: Keith Williams Architects

Athlone Art Gallery
Client: Athlone Town Council
Architect: Keith Williams Architects
Keith Williams, Richard Brown, Nicola Fox, Dan Lobato, Britta Neffgen
Structural Engineering: ARUP Consulting Engineers
M & E Engineering: AXIS Engineering
Archaeologist: Byrne Mullins and Associates
Quantity Surveyor: Mulgahy McDonach & Partners Ltd
Digital Imaging: Keith Williams Architects

Mosegård Museum of Cultural History
Client: Moesgård Museum
Architect: Keith Williams Architects
Keith Williams, Richard Brown, Stephen Clarke, Michael Rabe, Ingrid Sletten, Carl Trenfield
Structural Engineering: Buro Happold
M & E Engineering: Buro Happold
Cost Consultant: Davis Langdon
Digital Imaging: Keith Williams Architects
Aerial Photography: DDO, COPYRIGHT COWI

Kunstens Hus
Client: Herning Kunst Museum
Architect: Keith Williams Architects
Keith Williams, Richard Brown, Stephen Clarke, Ingrid Sletten, Carl Trenfield
Structural Engineering: ARUP
M & E Engineering: ARUP
Cost Consultant: Davis Langdon
Digital Imaging: Keith Williams Architects
Aerial Photography: DDO, COPYRIGHT COWI

Universität und Landesbibliothek TU Darmstadt
Client: TU Darmstadt
Architect: Keith Williams Architects
Keith Williams, Richard Brown, Stephen Clarke, Annika Grafweg, Carl Trenfield
Digital Imaging: Keith Williams Architects

Wexford Opera House

Client: Wexford Festival Opera

Project Manager: Office of Public Works on behalf of the Department of Arts, Sports and Tourism

Architect: OPW Architectural Services/Keith Williams Architects

OPW: Klaus Unger, Ciarán McGahon

Keith Williams Architects

Keith Williams, Richard Brown (director in charge), John Ahern, Ilex Beinemeier, Graham Bizley, Guy Davies, Sofia Kapsalis, Clayton Shortall, Michelle Wong, Philipp Macke, Ingrid Sletten, Carl Trenfield, Thorsten Werner

Acoustician: Arup Acoustics

Theatre Consultants: Carr & Angier

Structural Engineering: ARUP Consulting Engineers

M & E Engineering: OPW M + E Engineering

Fire Engineering: Brendan Harty & Associates

Lighting Consultants: Sutton Vane Associates

Cost Consultant: Nolan Ryan

Main Contractor: Cleary Doyle Contracting Ltd.

Digital Imaging: Keith Williams Architects

Photographers: Ros Kavanagh, Ger Lawlor, Pat Redmond

Chichester District Museum

Client: Chichester District Council

Project Manager: Robinson Low Francis

Architect: Keith Williams Architects

Keith Williams, Justin Holland (project architect), John Ahern, Sandra Beyer, Sascha Bischoff, Ilex Beinemeier, Cheah Yit Eet, James Davies, Britta Neffgen, Clayton Shortall, Ingrid Sletten, Thorsten Werner

Structural Engineering: Techniker

M & E Engineering: Gifford

Exhibitions: Event Communications

Lighting Consultants: Sutton Vane Associates

Archaeologist: Development Archaeology Services Ltd

Cost Consultant: Rider Levitt Bucknall

Digital Imaging: Keith Williams Architects

Models: Hidden Modelshop

Aerial Photography: Promap® Landmark Information Group [NB bold 'map']

Photograph of Archaeological Remains: ©Chichester District Council

Birmingham REP and the Birmingham City Library

Client: Birmingham REP & Birmingham City Council

Architect: Keith Williams Architects

Keith Williams, Richard Brown, Thorsten Werner

Digital Imaging: Keith Williams Architects

Aerial Photography: Promap® Landmark Information Group

Sculpture Building, Royal College of Art

Client: Royal College of Art

Architect: Keith Williams Architects

Keith Williams, Richard Brown, James Davies, Clayton Shortall, Ingrid Sletten

Structural Engineering: Buro Happold

M & E Engineering: Buro Happold

Digital Imaging: Keith Williams Architects

Models: Jackie Hands

Flekkefjord Kulturhus

Client: Flekkefjord Kommune

Architect: Keith Williams Architects

Keith Williams, Daniel Lobato, Ingrid Sletten, Carl Trenfield, Thorsten Werner

Digital Imaging: Keith Williams Architects

New Marlowe Theatre

Client: Canterbury City Council

Project Manager: Drivers Jonas

Architect: Keith Williams Architects

Keith Williams, Richard Brown (director in charge), Guy Davies (associate in charge – design stage), Matthew Green (project architect), John Ahern, Licia de Angelis, Sandra Beyer, Cheah Yit Eet, James Davies, Nicola Fox, Britta Neffgen, Mark Taylor, Carl Trenfield

Structural Engineering: Buro Happold

M & E Engineering: Max Fordham Consulting Engineers

Fire Engineering: Buro Happold: FEDRA

Acoustician: Sandy Brown Associates

Theatre Consultants: Charcoal Blue

Lighting Consultants: Max Fordham Consulting Engineers

Cost Consultant: Rider Levitt Bucknall

Main Contractor: ISG Jackson

Digital Imaging: Keith Williams Architects

Visual Impact Assessment: Miller Hare Limited

Models: Hidden Modelshop

Søfartsmuseum

Client: Handels- og Søfartsmuseet

Architect: Keith Williams Architects

Keith Williams, Daniel Lobato, Ingrid Sletten, Carl Trenfield

Digital Imaging: Keith Williams Architects

New Civic Centre, Crawley

Client: Grosvenor Developments & Crawley Town Council

Architect: Keith Williams Architects

Keith Williams, Richard Brown, Carl Trenfield

Digital Imaging: Keith Williams Architects

Molde Theatre and Jazzhouse

Client: Molde Kommune

Architect: Keith Williams Architects

Keith Williams, Ingrid Sletten, Nicola Fox, Carl Trenfield, Thorsten Werner

Digital Imaging: Keith Williams Architects

Residential Tower, 81 Black Prince Road

Client: Ristoia Ltd

Project Manager: KMCS

Architect: Keith Williams Architects

Keith Williams, Richard Brown (director in charge), Sascha Bischoff, Ilex Beinemeier, James Davies, Britta Neffgen, Michael Nettleship, Ludwig Steyl

Planning Consultant: DP9

Structural Engineering: Adams Kara Taylor

M & E Engineering: RYB Consult

Cost Consultant: KMCS

Digital Imaging: Keith Williams Architects

Architectural Visualisation: Miller Hare Limited

Models: Hidden Modelshop

Photographer: David Grandorge, Keith Williams Architects

Aerial Photography: Promap® Landmark Information Group

The Army Memorial, Athlone Castle

Client: Athlone Town Council

Architect: Keith Williams Architects

Keith Williams, Britta Neffgen, Clayton Shortall

Structural Engineering: ARUP Consulting Engineers

Quantity Surveyor: Mulgahy McDonach & Partners

Lighting Consultants: Sutton Vane Associates

Digital Imaging: Keith Williams Architects

Plot 8: Former Fire Station

Client: More London

Architect: Keith Williams Architects

Keith Williams, Ludwig Steyl (project architect), John Ahern, Ilex Beinemeier, Cheah Yit Eet, James Davies, Justin Holland, Michael Nettleship, Mark Taylor, Carl Trenfield

Structural Engineering: ARUP

M & E Engineering: ARUP

Planning Consultant: DP9

Historic Buildings Consultant: KM Heritage

Cost Consultant: EC Harris

Digital Imaging: Keith Williams Architects

More London Plot 7 background image supplied by Foster & Partners

NS-Dokumentationszentrum

Client:Landeshaupstadt München

Architect: Keith Williams Architects

Keith Williams, Richard Brown, Ilex Beinemeier, Sascha Bischoff, Britta Neffgen, Michael Nettleship, Ingrid Sletten, Carl Trenfield

M & E Engineering: Buro Happold

Landscape Architect: Anna Streitz

Digital Imaging: Keith Williams Architects

Plaine du Pal Urban Masterplan

Client: Mairie de Cahors, Cahors, France

Architect: Keith Williams

Engineer: ARUP

Digital Imaging: Keith Williams Architects

Campus de la Justicia de Madrid

Client: Campus de la Justicia de Madrid AS

Architect: Keith Williams Architects

Keith Williams, Richard Brown, Michael Rabe

Digital Imaging: Keith Williams Architects

Wembley 'Missing Link' Masterplan

Client: Brent Council & Stadium Housing Ltd

Architect: Keith Williams Architects

Keith Williams, Michael Nettleship

Digital Imaging: Keith Williams Architects

RGB Aerial Photography: ©GeoPerspectives Bluesky International Ltd.

Product: Ironmongery, The Parallel Range

Door handles manufactured in the UK by Ize Ltd.

Additional Photography Credits

Photographs on pages 5, 6 and back cover by James Cameron, www.jcameron.org

Index

Acknowledgments

A great many people have contributed to this monograph during the somewhat lengthy period that has elapsed since I first started thinking of setting out a comprehensive record of my work to date. I would like to extend my sincere thanks to each one of the firm's clients with whom we have worked over the years to create such special projects. To Kenneth Powell, with whom I first discussed the project in a Covent Garden restaurant a number of years back, and Paul Finch, each of whom has contributed such insightful text.

I should also like to thank Dr Sandra O'Connell for travelling from Dublin to interview me and for her concise record of our wide-ranging discussions; James Davies and Nicola Fox from my studio for redrawing and assembling with undimmed enthusiasm the graphic material and photography for publication;

my wife, Vanessa Shrimpton, for painstakingly proofreading and correcting my project texts; and all of the firm's staff, past and present, whose hard work has helped create our schemes, in particular my co-director, Richard Brown, who has been an important critic and influence in the development of so many of our projects.

My thanks also to the many consultants and engineers who have contributed to development of our work; to all who have given their permission for reproduction of the graphic material; and finally to editor Andrew Hall and The Images Publishing Group in Australia, for their collective patience and care during the many, many months that were needed for the preparation and finalisation of this book.

Keith R Williams